D. P. MORAN

Historical Association of Ireland
Life and Times Series, No. 4

D. P. Moran

PATRICK MAUME

Published for the
HISTORICAL ASSOCIATION OF IRELAND
By Dundalgan Press Ltd

First published 1995
ISBN 0-85221-125-2

© Patrick Maume 1995
Cover design: Jarlath Hayes
Cover illustration: Michael Healy
Historical Association of Ireland, Dublin
Printed by Dundalgan Press, Dundalk

FOREWORD

This series of short biographical studies published by the Historical Association of Ireland is designed to place the lives of leading historical figures against the background of new research on the problems and conditions of their times. These studies should be particularly helpful to students preparing for Leaving Certificate, G.C.E. Advanced Level and undergraduate history examinations, while at the same time appealing to the general public.

CIARAN BRADY
EUGENE J. DOYLE
Historical Association of Ireland

PREFACE

I began this book as a Junior Fellow at the Institute of Irish Studies at Queen's University, Belfast, and completed it as Assistant Lecturer in the Department of Modern Irish History, University College, Dublin. It owes much to my colleagues in both institutions, to Brian Walker, Valerie Hall and Jane Leonard, and to Mary Daly, Michael Laffan, Paul Bew, Tom Garvin, Alvin Jackson, J. J. Lee and Brian S. Murphy, who read an earlier draft and suggested improvements. I am solely responsible for the final product. Tom Dunne supervised earlier research involving Moran, which was also facilitated by Diarmuid Ó Gilleáin and Gearóid Ó Cruadhlaoich; the Irish History Students' Association and Irish Historical Society heard papers on him; Margaret O'Callaghan discussed him. Eugene Doyle and Ciaran Brady accepted my proposal to write on Moran. My family, as always, provided affection and support. I apologise for monopolising the departmental PC.

This book is dedicated to the memory of Dr Jerome Hayes.

PATRICK MAUME
Department of Modern Irish History
University College, Dublin

CONTENTS

CHRONOLOGY		1
INTRODUCTION		3
1.	Confessions of a Converted West Briton	6
2.	A Plea for Economics	13
3.	Twisting the Sourfaces, 1910–23	31
4.	The Philosophy of Independent Ireland, 1923–36	43
	CONCLUSION	53
	NOTES	57
	SELECT BIBLIOGRAPHY	62

CHRONOLOGY OF MORAN'S LIFE AND TIMES

1869 David Patrick Moran born in Waterford.

1870s At Christian Brothers' School, Waterford. Elder brothers Edward and Joseph involved in separatist activities.

1880–87 Follows Joseph to Castleknock. Edward associated with O'Donovan Rossa in America.

1887 Goes to London as journalist.

1890–91 Parnell split: a Parnellite activist and I.N.L. branch secretary.

1891–6 Drops out of politics. Continues journalistic career; acquires experience as editor. Attends London University economics courses.

1896 Joins London branch of Gaelic League.

1898 Revisits Ireland. Publishes first chapter of *The Philosophy of Irish Ireland* in *New Ireland Review*. Acquires Father Tom Finlay as patron.

1899 Returns to Dublin as freelance journalist. Plans new Irish Ireland journal with Munster faction of League. Tours Munster Gaeltacht.

1900 *Leader* prospectus distributed (summer). First issue of *Leader* (1 September). Irish Party reunited.

1901 Marries Teresa O'Toole (5 children: 4 sons and a daughter, Nuala). Coins the nicknames 'Sourface', 'Saved' and 'Idolator'.

1902 Anti-discrimination campaign. Catholic Association founded. Arthur Clery first writes for *Leader*.

1903 'Collar the King' policy. Establishment of Cork and Dublin Industrial Development Associations.

1904 Griffith publishes *The Resurrection of Hungary*. Father Michael O'Riordan serialises *Catholicity and Progress* in *Leader*. Catholic Association eclipsed.

1905 *The Philosophy of Irish Ireland* published as book. *Tom O'Kelly* published. Young Ireland Branch founded. Arthur Clery first advocates partition.

1907 Synge's *Playboy of the Western World*. Clery's *Idea of a Nation*.

1909 Controversy over compulsory Irish in National University of Ireland.

1910 Irish Party acquires balance of power at Westminster.

1912 Literature crusade: Vigilance Committees established. Home Rule Bill introduced.

1913–14 Moran advocates Belfast boycott and Irish Volunteers.

1914 Outbreak of First World War. Moran opposes recruiting.

1916 *Leader* offices destroyed in Easter Rising.

2 D. P. MORAN

1917 Rise of Sinn Féin: Moran supports it after East Clare by-election.
1918 Conscription crisis. War ends. 1918 general election: victory of Sinn Féin.
1919 Dáil Éireann meets. Nuala Moran begins writing for *Leader*. *Leader* suppressed (August). Resumes publication as *New Leader*, Joseph Dolan nominal proprietor.
1920 *Leader* resumes original title. Clery's *Dublin Essays*. Clery appointed Sinn Féin judge.
1921 Truce (June). Anglo-Irish Treaty (December). Moran and most contributors (except Clery) support Treaty.
1922–3 Civil War.
1923 Moran adopts protectionism.
1926 Sinn Féin split: Moran expects political realignment.
1927 Fianna Fáil main opposition party: acquires support of many protectionists. Death of 'Imaal'.
1928 Moran endorses Fianna Fáil.
1929 Deaths of Moran's two eldest sons (January and April).
1930 Moran reverts to Cumann na nGaedheal over Fianna Fáil ambivalence on constitutional issue.
1932 Fianna Fáil election victory: Moran votes Cumann na nGaedheal but welcomes protectionist measures. Death of Arthur Clery. Blueshirts founded.
1933 Fianna Fáil overall majority. Moran fiercely hostile owing to Economic War and I.R.A. activity. Fears Fianna Fáil dictatorship; endorses Eoin O'Duffy.
1934 Local elections dispel hope of speedy Fianna Fáil downfall. Opposition split. Deaths of William Dawson and Father Dinneen.
1936 Death of D. P. Moran (1 February). Nuala succeeds him as editor and proprietor of *Leader*.
1940s *Leader* becomes a fortnightly.
1950s *Leader* revived under influence of T. Desmond Williams.
1960s *Leader* becomes a monthly.
1971 *Leader* ceases publication.

INTRODUCTION

The political disputes which convulsed Irish life between the Land War and the Treaty provoked intense intellectual debate. Catholics, Protestants and pagans, separatist and parliamentarian nationalists, moderate and hardline Unionists struggled to shape the future. Should Ireland be linked to the British Empire? What role would the ex-landlords and the business classes play in the new Ireland? What was to become of the Ulster Unionists? Was Protestant domination of Irish business due to anti-Catholic discrimination, and what could be done about it? Were Protestants and Unionists compatriots to be conciliated, or alien enemies to be subjugated? Were the Irish overseas part of the Irish nation, or lost to it forever? How should Irish Catholicism respond to the new challenges facing it? What was to be the role of women in the new Ireland? Did Ireland's economic future lie with industrial development, a more efficient agriculture, or with a self-sufficient peasantry? Should Ireland be socialist or capitalist, or something in between? Could the Irish language be saved, and how? Could Irish identity survive without it? Could there be an Irish national literature in English? How much freedom should the individual artist be allowed? Could the Irish Parliamentary Party avoid either disintegration or the tyranny of an unaccountable leadership?

Near the centre of many of these debates stand D. P. Moran and his weekly paper *The Leader*. Moran has attracted scholarly attention as an aggressive and articulate exponent of a Catholic Gaelic vision of Irish identity, summed up in his slogans 'Irish Ireland' and 'The Gael must be the element that absorbs'. Such analyses usually concentrate on his early manifesto *The Philosophy of Irish Ireland*. There has been no attempt to work through *The Leader* from its foundation in September 1900 until Moran's death in February 1936.

Moran is generally depicted using remarkable journalistic talents to spread bigotry and sectarian hatred: leading the mob

3

against Yeats and the Abbey Theatre; trying to make the Gaelic League a Catholic organisation; attacking Protestants as 'Sourfaces' and moderate nationalists as 'West Britons'. Much of this picture of Moran is true, but it is not the whole truth. Moran is too often seen in isolation. Concentration on his manifesto rather than his paper conceals his success in recruiting talented contributors (who were not Moran clones) and his willingness to open his pages to opposing viewpoints. The cultural historians who have studied Moran neglect his entrepreneurial activities—the business strategies which made *The Leader* successful, and the role of the paper in the wider industrial movement of the period.

Moran's bigotry, entrepreneurship and cultural revivalism cannot be separated; they belonged to the same agenda. He spoke for Catholic professionals and small businessmen forcing their way into economic sectors dominated by Protestant and Unionist patronage networks. Sections of Protestant opinion responded to this development by sectarian statements and campaigns. Moran's bigotry was partly a response to this Protestant backlash. This is an explanation, not an excuse: other Catholics and nationalists tried to avoid sectarianism, just as some Protestants and Unionists tried to avoid committing themselves to blind defence of existing privilege.

Before 1914 Moran was often critical of the Irish Parliamentary Party, but was even more hostile to separatists. Some younger and more vigorous elements of the party used *The Leader* as a platform and co-operated with its cultural and economic campaigns. Study of *The Leader* modifies the view that the Irish Party had entirely lost touch with the new Irish Ireland movements or that industrial revivalists generally supported Sinn Féin; it also shows that the xenophobia, censorship mentality and Gaelic chauvinism which disfigured the post-independence state were present before 1914. Most accounts of Moran end in 1916, but his activities in the 1920s and 1930s show how the tariff issue led much of the business class to transfer its loyalties to de Valera's Fianna Fáil party, and how this related to other issues.

The urban Catholic middle classes of Moran's day have been eclipsed by middle-class secularisation since the 1960s and the demise of many established Irish firms (including *The Leader* itself) after the end of protectionism. Moran is a creature of a vanished world, but also at times a remarkably modern-sounding commentator; some of his ideas are still heard today. This book discusses his life and projects, how far he succeeded, and whether he failed.

1

CONFESSIONS OF A CONVERTED WEST BRITON

David Patrick Moran was born in Waterford in 1869, the son of James Moran, a building contractor. D.P. had at least two elder brothers and one sister (she married a local man called Poole).[1] Edward Moran, about twenty-five years older than David, was a solicitor in Waterford in the 1870s and joined a literary society which included Richard Dowling and Edmund Downey (later well-known popular novelists) and Thomas Sexton (afterwards a leading Home Rule M.P.). Edward emigrated to America and associated with the Fenian leader O'Donovan Rossa. In 1883 he travelled to Britain to act as a defence lawyer for the killer of the informer James Carey. Edward ghost-wrote a novel published under Rossa's name in 1884. The novel is set in County Waterford, near Fethard; it denounces landlord tyranny, condones the shooting of landlords, and advocates armed rebellion. Edward Moran practised law in Brooklyn until his death in 1914.[2]

Joseph Moran, a few years older than David, initially took after Edward. One night in the late 1870s he was discovered drilling with some boys. Whether this was simply a boyish game or linked to some organisation, his parents sent him away to the Vincentian Fathers' College at Castleknock, near Dublin. David followed a few years later. He was a quiet, athletic pupil, pious like his brother.[3] D.P. later ridiculed 'Cawstleknock' for its pretensions to gentility.

As a boy D.P. 'enjoyed a sound National education outside school hours', reading the romantic nationalist literature of the time (though also the satirical serial *Mick M'Quaid*), knowing *Speeches from the Dock* by heart, enraptured by the flamboyant speeches of the Nationalist M.P. William O'Brien, dreaming of a new '98 Rising and patriotic death on the scaffold. The adolescent Moran despised emigration as unpatriotic, but secretly felt that any lad of spirit would emigrate if given the chance. The hero of his novel *Tom O'Kelly* engages in similar self-deception.[4]

Tom O'Kelly emigrates because his father ruins the family business through involvement in politics, and thereby in drink. (Politics involved recreation as much as ideology; pubs were favourite political meeting-places.) Whether or not this happened in the Moran family (which might explain Moran's lifelong hostility to 'Mr Bung' the publican), they could probably give their younger sons little more than a good education and some contacts. Joseph and D.P. went to London as journalists. In 1887 D.P. began work on T. P. O'Connor's new evening paper, *The Star*.

D.P. took every opportunity to defy the Saxon, 'risking my prospects by palliating boycotting and extreme forms of national endeavour'. Gradually he realised that the Saxon was puzzled, ignorant, and uninterested in Ireland. D.P. realised that by worrying about what the Saxon thought, he had mistaken grovelling for defiance and had made a fool of himself.

London was much bigger and wealthier, and the British armed forces stronger and better equipped, than Moran had imagined. He realised that when he dreamed Ireland might defeat Britain in the 1890s because she had nearly done so in the 1790s, he was like a huckster thinking that because he once competed on equal terms with a neighbouring huckster, he could compete with a monster store. 'Economic forces sway the world now.'[5]

Both brothers were active in the Irish National League. At the time of the Parnell split Moran was secretary of an I.N.L. branch. He brought it over to Parnellism and became an active Parnellite, vociferously anticlerical. He had literary ambitions; he showed friends unpublished poems and an early version of *Tom O'Kelly*.[6] After Parnell's death Moran saw the futility of the split. Joseph remained politically active, but D.P. dropped out of politics, hating the prospect of becoming an Englishman by adoption, yet convinced that Ireland was doomed. He cultivated contempt for the English and sardonic detachment from the Irish.

Over the next few years Moran took two London University extension courses in economics—one given by Sidney Webb, the other by the social Darwinist W. S. Armytage Smith. He absorbed the social Darwinism of the British movement for 'national efficiency'. He became a drama critic, and caused a stir by saying

8   D. P. MORAN

exactly what he thought about plays; he also worked on a land reform paper and later edited a small London local paper.[7]

In 1896 Fionán Mac Coluim, founder of the London branch of the Gaelic League, invited Moran to a language class. Moran was reluctant. As a boy he had heard rhetoric about ancient glories and had tried to learn Irish from a textbook, but he soon gave up for lack of support and never fully realised that Brian Boru and Red Hugh O'Donnell did not speak English. After seeing the gap between romantic rhetoric and political squabbles, he suspected that the Irish were savages before the English came.

Twenty minutes into the language class, Moran thought: 'Well, damn them for Sassenachs, here is one thing we have got that they haven't!' Here was the lost key to his stubborn feeling that in spite of everything 'thou shalt be Irish, thou shalt not be English'. The romantic nationalism of his boyhood, the political activities of his youth were clumsy imitations. All his life he had been a West Briton without knowing it.[8] Moran set about learning Irish, though he habitually disrupted classes with practical jokes and smart remarks.[9]

This development strained relations with his brother Joseph. Joseph saw no great merit in the Irish language and decided that while he would always be a Catholic and an Irish nationalist, he lived in England and must make the best of it. Joseph spent the rest of his life as a London journalist and political activist. D.P. Moran was determined to avoid such a fate.[10]

Late in 1898 opportunity presented itself. After a visit to Ireland Moran wrote about his impressions for the *New Ireland Review*, an intellectual monthly associated with the Jesuit-run University College in Dublin. The editor, Father Tom Finlay, asked Moran to make it a series. From December 1898 to early 1900 Moran outlined his interpretation of Irish history and society; in 1905 the articles appeared in book form as *The Philosophy of Irish Ireland*.

Moran lamented that by identifying with Grattan's Parliament the native Irish abandoned their identity for a sham; that Davis compounded the sham by proclaiming an all-creeds-and-classes version of Irish nationality which never existed outside the imaginations of dreamers; that O'Connell, though he raised the people from their knees, by flattering them to raise their self-confidence made them see flattery as their entitlement and honest criticism as enmity; that the nationalist movement failed to produce any coherent analysis of Irish society, reduced nationality to politics, and held that nothing could be done until political freedom was gained—with the result that the typical middle-class nationalist (lacking any solid focus for his nationalism) went from adolescent fantasy to middle-aged sloganeering to 'Castle Catholic' social climbing.

Moran did not condemn snobbery as such. He accepted it as inevitable and wanted to use it. (He tried to Gaelicise the colleges, not to abolish them; his daughter went to Muckross College, the most Irish Ireland girls' school in Dublin.) He called the Irish 'feminine'—emotional, reactive, and irresponsible; he wanted them 'masculine'—strong, self-confident and assertive. (A *Leader* cartoonist portrayed Moran's symbol of Ireland: a powerful male nude grappling with the serpent of Anglicisation.)[11] Then, instead of crawling after West Britons and imitating their vices, the native Irish would take pride in their (Catholic) religion and develop their sense of identity; instead of draining their businesses to put their sons into overcrowded professions and send their daughters to convent schools teaching useless fripperies, they would put their offspring into trade and build up the Irish economy. Moran's denunciations of pubs, gambling and music-halls are linked to his desire to implant a work-ethic in the Irish petty bourgeoisie. Moran's version of economic nationalism is distinguished from its contemporaries—United Irish League agrarianism, Griffithite protectionism—by its emphasis on human capital, its belief that natural resources are less important than the ability, determination and technical skills needed to use them. 'If only the farmers' heads were tilled their fields would soon follow.'

Moran maintained that the Irish could never compete with the English on equal terms in English literature or politics; they must fall back on Ireland and create there cultural and economic forces England could not ignore. 'Once Ireland had Home Power she could laugh at those who would deny her Home Rule.' The Gael must absorb the Anglo-Irish tradition or be absorbed—as Moran was almost absorbed in London.

In 1899 Moran returned to Ireland. He freelanced for the Healyite *Daily Nation*. (This was not as strange behaviour for a

10   D. P. MORAN

Parnellite as it may seem. The Redmondite wing of Parnellism had allied with Healy in self-protection against the United Irish League, founded by William O'Brien to force political reunion through a new land agitation.)

Moran took a cycling holiday through south-western Ireland, visiting Ballingeary and spending Christmas in Ballyferriter. He was impressed by the people and in later life increasingly romanticised his memories of his only visit to the Gaeltacht; but he noted how the North Cork Gaeltacht began where the railway ended and ended where it resumed. In his *New Ireland Review* articles Moran noted that the Gaelic revival was not a spontaneous self-renewal of the surviving Gaeltacht culture. The Irish language survived in the Gaeltacht only because these areas were backward and remote. The inhabitants were too demoralised to produce any serious movement, had no conscious attachment to the language, and discarded it as soon as they could. (*The Leader* periodically denounced 'the Irish-speaking slave'—the native speaker who refused to speak Irish.)

Moran emphasised that the Gaelic League was an urban movement, founded by English-speakers who realised that Irish identity depended on the language. The struggle would be decided in the towns. Moran argued in *An Claideamh Soluis* that the League could not be a purely cultural movement; without national revivalism few would study Irish culture for its own sake. The Gaelic League was non-political, but still nationalist; nationality was above politics.[12]

This was the view of a townsman neither familiar with Gaelic folk culture nor interested in classical Irish literature. (Moran eventually read modern Irish fluently, though he never spoke it well; but he rarely went beyond An tAthair Peadar Ó Laoghaire's popular novel *Séadna*.)[13] Moran allied with the dissident League faction which favoured Munster Irish and an explicit nationalist policy and opposed co-operation with the Pan-Celts. He joined the Keating Branch (Dublin base and national centre of the dissidents) when it was established. Of the Munster leaders, An tAthair Peadar Ó Laoghaire and Father Patrick S. Dinneen became regular contributors to *The Leader* (Dinneen became a personal friend), while P. J. Keawell worked with Moran in the Catholic Association.[14]

The dissidents wanted Moran as editor of an English-language weekly official organ of the League. When the leadership pre-empted this by establishing *An Claideamh Soluis*, Moran planned his own weekly. In the summer of 1900 he distributed a prospectus for the forthcoming publication, to be entitled *The Leader*.

His principal backer, apart from the Gaelic League dissidents, was Father Finlay, who was involved in numerous movements, notably Sir Horace Plunkett's attempt to improve Irish agriculture through co-operative methods. The University College Jesuits allegedly encouraged the new paper as a rival to Griffith's *United Irishman* (seen as dangerously anticlerical).[15] Some old acquaintances ridiculed Moran's remarkable growth in piety since the Parnell split.

This was unjust. Nationalists often combined intense religious devotion with political hostility to the clergy. Moran had been pious as a boy, and his daughter remembered him as deeply pious in later life. Finlay probably influenced Moran's initial favourable attitude towards Plunkett and perhaps encouraged students to write for *The Leader*, but he could not prevent Moran eventually turning against Plunkett or (much later) attacking Finlay's own economic ideas. *The Leader* was popular among Gaelic League seminarians and curates, but so fiercely attacked religious orders and clerical managers who excluded Irish from their schools that even Hyde feared it might endanger clerical support for the League.[16]

Moran clearly played down certain aspects of his views. Sometimes he engaged in a 'double-take'. He initially praised Plunkett's book *Ireland in the New Century*, while disagreeing with its criticism of the economic influence of the Catholic Church; but when Cardinal Logue led an outcry against Plunkett, *The Leader* attacked 'Sir Horace Shallow'. In the 1909 controversy over the dismissal of Dr Michael O'Hickey from his Maynooth professorship for attacking the bishops' attitude to compulsory Irish, the League leadership denounced the hierarchy, while *The Leader* warned against attacking the bishops (this also reflects the factional divide within the League). Moran combined personal piety with a cautious eye on clerical politics and dislike of dangerous theological speculation.

If Moran received financial help, it was probably in the form of loans rather than shareholdings. Moran's articles had drawn attention: he would be the new paper's principal asset. For the rest of his life he was sole and unfettered proprietor; this suggests that his savings provided the start-up capital. ('If it failed, I could always emigrate again.')

A few months after the launch of *The Leader* Moran married Teresa O'Toole, daughter of a retired sea captain who had been Parnellite Mayor of Waterford.[17] Probably they had known each other for some time and the date of their marriage depended on the success of *The Leader.*

2

A PLEA FOR ECONOMICS

The Leader appeared on 1 September 1900 and was an immediate success. Each week for several weeks the paper reported that the previous issue had sold out and that the print-run was being increased; a special horse and cart was engaged to supply newsagents.[1] This success was due to Moran's vigorous writing and candid criticism, and to effective marketing. (Moran had secured an able young business manager, Kevin Kenny, who later founded what was to become the biggest advertising agency in Dublin.)[2] *The Leader* was sustained by a systematic pursuit of Irish advertising and by attracting a wide range of writers and commentators.

Moran saw the publicising of Irish goods as one of *The Leader*'s roles. He defended 'Buy Irish' campaigns against doctrinaire free-traders, claiming that the Irish people were irrationally biased against Irish goods, but he held that it was futile to run Irish industries on sentiment. Irish people would only buy Irish goods 'as good and cheap' as imports. He admitted the faults of Irish manufacturers, particularly neglect of modern publicity methods. Moran satirised Irish manufacturers as 'Dark Brothers', a secret society hiding themselves from the public. He regularly visited factories and described then in *The Leader*. (Towards the end of his life he deputed the task to one M. J. Cranley.) Moran insisted that he took no payment for these articles (he denounced 'Mean Brothers' who benefited from *Leader* publicity without buying advertisements), but they nevertheless gave him contacts among the business community and made *The Leader* the paper of choice for Irish Irelanders looking for Irish goods and Irish manufacturers looking for customers. Within a few months *The Leader* regularly contained eight pages of advertisements. For the rest of his life Moran could refuse advertisements of which he disapproved (e.g. for most English imports—particularly English newspapers—and risqué plays) and attacked the Dublin nationalist dailies for not doing likewise. Moran boasted he had made *The*

13

14   D. P. MORAN

Leader a success on the principle 'as good and cheap' and jeered at the 'toy papers' established by William O'Brien and Arthur Griffith as political mouthpieces rather than business propositions.

Similarly, Moran attacked the Gaelic League leadership for not employing professional business managers. *An Claideamh Soluis* retorted by accusing Moran of name-calling, sectarianism, and publishing too few articles in Irish.[3] (Since *The Leader* wanted to convert English-speakers to Irish, which Moran believed would take two generations, it printed only one Irish-language article a week. Its most prominent Irish-language contributors were Ó Laoghaire, Dinneen, and Seán Ó Ciarghusa.) During the League's annual Language Procession in 1905, Moran was attacked by leadership supporters and narrowly escaped injury.[4]

Moran supported the Industrial Development Associations established in various Irish towns from 1903 onwards. These represented small and medium-sized enterprises rather than the bigger and older concerns which dominated the Chambers of Commerce. Moran attacked the 'Chambers of Importers' as representing distributors rather than manufacturers, and as concerns run by Protestant Unionists with a few West British Catholics like William Martin Murphy. (Murphy was a regular target of Moran's, whose scorn was especially directed at 'Murphy's ha'penny dreadful', the *Irish Independent*.) Moran was on particularly friendly terms with Joseph Milroy and Miss E. N. Somers (president and secretary of the Dublin I.D.A.), Kevin Kenny (also active in the Dublin I.D.A.), and a group of Cork industrialists who dominated the Cork I.D.A. These included the brothers J. C. and T. P. Dowdall, margarine manufacturers; Andrew O'Shaughnessy, founder of Dripsey Woollen Mills, and his manager William Cronin (who wrote for *The Leader* as 'Liam').

Moran's economic ideas encouraged his distrust of the United Irish League and the reunited Irish Party. The U.I.L. paid lip-service to the Irish language, but its rallies in Irish-speaking districts were conducted in English. Moran attacked the U.I.L. agrarian programme (land division) as economically naïve and irrelevant to urban Ireland. He criticised the prominence of publicans in it and its use by small-town hucksters against

A PLEA FOR ECONOMICS 15

Plunkett's attempt to set up co-operative stores. Plunkett was Unionist M.P. for South Dublin; Moran said that although Plunkett was a Unionist, he did more for Ireland than most of his nationalist critics. *The Leader* even endorsed Plunkett's Unionist candidacies for South Dublin in 1900 (where he was opposed by a hardline Independent Unionist who gave the Nationalists the seat on a split vote) and Galway City in 1901. Some nationalists even claimed that Moran was in Plunkett's pay.[5]

Moran also attacked the dictatorial leadership (accompanied by bombastic emotional oratory—'*ráiméis*'—and floods of personal abuse) exercised over the U.I.L. by the hero of his adolescence, William O'Brien. In *Tom O'Kelly* the futile political split between Twaddleites and Tweedleites is the O'Brien–Healy dispute of 1899–1900; the posturing Twaddleite leader, John Francis Xavier High Faluter, is O'Brien.[6] Moran called O'Brien a petty tyrant seeking the dictatorship which could only be exercised successfully by a greater man—Parnell—and which had created a crippling boycott mentality and plunged the country into chaos when the despot fell. Moran said the country was now too free and too well educated to tolerate such leadership. He called for the retirement of O'Brien and his ally John Dillon (seen as 'a political fossil' excessively influenced by British Radicalism) and the English-based T. P. O'Connor (his religious beliefs were vague, and he wrote gossip for cheap English newspapers). Moran wanted a Healy–Redmond leadership—debaters, not mob orators.

The Leader claimed to provide a new sort of leadership based on open criticism and debate. Moran welcomed clashes of opinion because he liked fighting for fighting's sake—and they increased circulation. The first issues were written almost entirely by Moran, and he always wrote several pages on current affairs, but other contributors soon appeared. They often used pen-names or initials (a widespread contemporary practice), but the identity of many was well known.

W. P. Ryan and P. D. Kenny ('Pat') were regular contributors until they founded the *Irish Peasant*, became increasingly anticlerical, and quarrelled with the church. Another early recruit was J. J. O'Toole ('Imaal'), a civil servant cousin of Jenny Wyse Power. 'Imaal' was an aggressively Catholic controversialist (he mellowed as he grew older), rather conservative, well-read and genuinely

16   D. P. MORAN

fond of literature. He became one of *The Leader*'s best-known contributors.[7]

The Literary and Historical (debating) Society of University College produced another group. Several contributed for a short time (including the future Chief Justice of the Irish Free State, Hugh Kennedy, who wrote under the pen-name 'Kappa Mega').[8] Two were of lasting importance to *The Leader*. These were Arthur Clery ('Chanel') and William Dawson ('Avis').

Dawson, who worked for the Land Commission, was the son of a former Home Rule M.P. and Lord Mayor of Dublin. He had affectionate childhood memories of Parnell and was also a celebrated Dublin wit. Most of his contributions to *The Leader* are satirical skits, notably a long-running series, 'As Others See Us', allegedly letters by an Englishman living in Ireland. Dawson's wit blended with Parnellite nostalgia. He once wrote a little fantasy about Parnell's return.[9]

Dawson's cousin Arthur Clery was the most important contributor to *The Leader* after Moran himself. An only child, raised by relatives after his mother died and his father took up a legal position in India, Clery had a complex personality with strong strains of cynicism, melancholy and shyness. In youth Clery admired Thackeray, and even after conversion to Irish Ireland based his advocacy of populism and folk-art on a semi-flippant doctrinaire rationalism (visible in an exchange with his fellow-student James Joyce about national drama).[10] This produced many absurdities. His distrust of Protestants and Freemasons was expressed with singular openness; a streak of self-pitying paranoia became noticeable as time passed.

Clery nevertheless had many personal and intellectual virtues. He supported female suffrage on religious grounds. He opposed corporal punishment, and even suggested that the voting age should be lowered to twelve. Clery was not antisemitic; he admired Belloc but denounced his 'wicked' writings against the Jews. As a barrister at the Four Courts, Clery befriended Indian law students. As a part-time law professor in University College, Dublin, he was widely respected for his friendliness towards students (rare among professors at the time).[11]

Clery made considerable sacrifices for his beliefs. In 1908 he turned down a well-paid American legal post because he dis-

A PLEA FOR ECONOMICS 17

approved of emigration. (Perhaps he was influenced by resentment at his father.) He could never afford to marry; he lived austerely (apart from a fondness for visits to the continent) and spent his money on his students and charitable work in the slums with the St Vincent de Paul Society.[12]

A third major contributor came from the same 'L. & H.' milieu, but did not write for Moran regularly until after 1910. Louis J. Walsh, son of a Land Leaguer in Maghera, County Londonderry, and brother of the writer and future T.D., Helena Concannon, clashed with Joyce at U.C.D. Walsh denounced Joyce as un-national; Joyce sneered at Walsh's conventional and sentimental writings.[13] Walsh became a solicitor in Ballycastle, County Antrim, active in the Gaelic League and in the U.I.L. until 1914, when he broke with the party over partition. In 1918 he contested South Londonderry for Sinn Féin. After the Treaty he became a District Justice in Donegal, while commenting freely on public affairs in *The Leader*, the *Irish Rosary* and local journals. He was a strong advocate of censorship. Walsh's writing combines observation of Ulster society with sentimentalism and political propaganda.

Walsh is an intermediate figure between the metropolitan and provincial contributors, as is Daniel Corkery. Corkery began as one of many dissatisfied provincials whom Moran encouraged to write to *The Leader* describing local petty snobbery and Anglicisation, but in time he developed into a major contributor. Moran believed Corkery's critical intelligence appeared more fully in his *Leader* articles than in his better-known work.[14]

Many provincial contributors are unidentifiable, but a group of mid-western priests deserves attention. Bishop Fogarty of Killaloe read *The Leader* regularly, sent messages of support, and praised it in a pastoral. (Fogarty attended Moran's funeral.)[15] Bishop O'Dwyer of Limerick is also said to have admired *The Leader*.[16]

Two prominent Limerick priests and O'Dwyer associates wrote for *The Leader*. Father Michael O'Riordan, based in Limerick city, wore several polemical serials in its early years, notably a lengthy rebuttal of Sir Horace Plunkett's views about the influence of Catholicism on the Irish economy. O'Riordan's critique, republished as a book (*Catholicity and Progress in Ireland*) was allegedly

18 D. P. MORAN

responsible for his appointment as President of the Irish College in Rome (where he served until his death in 1920).

Moran's other important Limerick ally was Dean Denis Hallinan of Newcastlewest. Hallinan was active in the Gaelic League, set an hour aside each day to learn Irish, and became a fluent speaker. Hallinan also wrote for the *Catholic Bulletin*. In 1914, like Bishop O'Dwyer and Moran, he took an anti-recruiting stance and later supported Sinn Féin. In January 1918 Hallinan succeeded O'Dwyer as Bishop of Limerick. He died in 1923.[17]

Neither O'Riordan nor Hallinan were of the same intellectual calibre as Moran and his best metropolitan contributors. Great claims have been made for *Catholicity and Progress*,[18] but it is badly structured, ambivalent about economic development, and refuses to admit any truth in Plunkett's views even where similar comments were made by unimpeachably Catholic nationalists (including Moran).

Hallinan's limitations appear in a *Leader* controversy about Carnegie libraries. Hallinan and another Limerick correspondent wanted Carnegie libraries to be rejected in favour of parish libraries, because, since Protestants could not be excluded from Carnegie libraries, it would be impossible to veto books considered unsuitable for Catholics, and Catholics could not then be kept from reading them. (This anticipates the 1930 Mayo library controversy.) Moran and 'Imaal', living in Dublin where the allegedly dangerous material was far more accessible than in rural Limerick, pointed out that people could not be shielded indefinitely from such material, and that the benefits of reading outweighed the risks.[19]

Moran's clerical and white-collar lay readers were united in resentment at the way the business community and upper reaches of the civil service were dominated by Protestants, who maintained their position through patronage networks such as the Freemasons. This aspect of pre-independence Irish life, ignored by many historians, helps to explain the appeal of nationalism to white-collar Catholic workers. (A related grievance was the transfer of British civil servants to Irish positions; anyone interested in Ernest Gellner's theory that nationalism is related to the desire of the educated classes of the submerged nation to carve out a

A PLEA FOR ECONOMICS 19

sphere of influence free from metropolitan competition might read Moran's diatribes against 'English dumps'.)[20]

From the beginning Moran denounced the practice of glossing over the fact that the vast majority of nationalists were Catholics, while most Protestants were Unionists. He said that Protestants could be Irish, but that they must realise that Ireland was a Catholic country; he poured scorn on those who praised Protestant Home Rulers 'because they had the common decency to be nationalists'. He jeered at such 'tame Catholics' as servile 'tolerance provers'.

From its inception *The Leader* published articles on anti-Catholic discrimination. Early in 1902 it launched a major campaign, beginning with the Great Southern and Western Railway, extending to other railway companies and banks, and then to other Protestant-owned businesses. *The Leader* published analyses of the personnel employed in selected companies, showing extreme Protestant over-representation among clerical staff. Some of these articles were published as a pamphlet, *Three Railways and a Bank*. (Railways and banks constituted longstanding grievances to economic nationalists. Banks were accused of failure to invest in Irish industry, railways of using their monopoly position to impose excessive freight charges on small-scale exporters while giving bulk discounts to large-scale importers. Moran linked these preferences to the proprietors' religious and political outlook.)

Moran and like-minded individuals (notably Dean Hallinan, the ex-M.P. and future Sinn Féin President John Sweetman, the veteran Cork Parnellite M. J. Horgan and his son J. J. Horgan—a *Leader* contributor and Irish Party activist—and Michael Sullivan, an elderly lawyer active in exposing discrimination by Unionist-dominated Rathmines Council) bought railway shares and protested at shareholders' meetings. These meetings were reported in *The Leader*, with exhortations to Catholic shareholders to take action. Sir William Goulding, fertiliser manufacturer and prominent Unionist and Freemason, who sat on the boards of several of the companies involved, was a particular target. The protestors called for clerks to be chosen by competitive examination rather than directors' nomination. This was conceded after Nationalist M.P.s blocked railway legislation in the House of Commons.

20 D. P. MORAN

The campaign helped to create the Catholic Association in November 1902. The association is often presented as a Healyite front. In fact its founders were a mixture of Moran's campaigners, Healy associates and Catholic Actionists desiring a federation of Catholic societies. Prominent members included Father Tom Finlay and Kevin Kenny. Infighting and reckless calls for exclusive trading by Catholics led to its censure by Archbishop Walsh, but a nucleus survived as the Catholic Defence Society and later became the Knights of St Columbanus.[21]

The railway agitation alarmed many Protestants. Some Protestants attributed Catholic under-representation to native incompetence and/or inefficient Catholic education; others complained that Protestants could not compete with Catholic boys specially drilled for examinations. Others spoke of the thin end of a wedge aimed at excluding Protestants by compulsory Irish. (This was a shrewd prediction. Moran regularly called for Irish to be given more weight in the examination; when the Free State government amalgamated the railways, Irish was made compulsory for employees.)[22]

Objections were not confined to Unionists. The nationalist Church of Ireland Canon J. O. Hannay (better known by his pseudonym 'George A. Birmingham') attacked the campaign in his novel *Hyacinth*; he admitted that discrimination existed, but objected to all Protestants being held collectively responsible. The socialist, separatist and agnostic Frederick Ryan declared that protestors should oppose discrimination as citizens rather than Catholics and remarked that they did not oppose discrimination in general, since Moran supported the boycott against Limerick Jews.[23]

The campaign included an offensive against Protestant assumptions of cultural and religious superiority. Shortly after Queen Victoria died, Moran took the Rathmines tram home from his office. (He lived in Pembroke, near the Rathmines boundary. Rathmines and Pembroke were independent townships with a large Protestant middle-class population and Unionist-controlled councils.) Moran gazed at the long faces in the tram, ostentatiously sorrowing for the dead queen, and coined his most famous nickname: 'Sourface'. Ostensibly, 'Sourface' stood for a particular affectation of superiority, and Moran repeatedly denied that it

A PLEA FOR ECONOMICS

meant 'Protestant'. It was sometimes applied to Catholic Unionists; but such people were called 'Catholic Sourfaces', thereby implying that Sourfaces are normally Protestant.[24]

Moran soon produced an explicitly sectarian nickname. When *The Leader* was founded, concessions to Catholics and nationalists by Conservative administrations created a hardline populist backlash among rank-and-file Unionists. Lindsay Crawford's paper the *Irish Protestant,* the ex-Catholic publicist Michael MacCarthy and the Belfast lay street-preachers and political demagogues Arthur Trew and T. H. Sloan accused the Dublin Castle administration of pandering to the Catholic Church and attributed all Ireland's social, political and economic woes to clerical tyranny. (Plunkett's 1900 defeat was a product of the backlash; he was denounced by Protestant extremists—only to be then attacked as one of those same extremists by Catholic and nationalist critics.)[25]

The traditional accession declaration of British monarchs called the doctrine of transubstantiation 'idolatrous and blasphemous'. Edward VII thought this offensive, and there was talk of amending it. Protestant extremists said that even a monarch who was a lifelong Anglican and swore to uphold the Church of England might be a secret papist unless he insulted Roman Catholicism in terms which any Roman Catholic would think unforgivable. The declaration remained; Moran promptly described himself and his fellow-Catholics as 'Idolators' and called Protestants 'anti-Idolators' or 'the Saved' (Evangelical Protestant believe those who have been 'born again' are certain of salvation). At the time of the accession of George V in 1910, Moran said Catholics should list themselves as 'Idolators' in the census unless the declaration was amended. (It was amended.)

Moran and the Protestant extremists encouraged one another. Moran quoted the diatribes of MacCarthy and 'our funny contemporary *The Irish Protestant*' as representing Protestant opinion towards Catholics. He highlighted Orange speeches and the activities of Protestant missionary societies in the Dublin slums. Crawford quoted *The Leader* as proof of Catholic intolerance, and the Catholic Association was called a clerical conspiracy to deprive Protestants of employment. When the Limerick Jews were boycotted in 1904, Unionist hardliners claimed that moderate

22 D. P. MORAN

Chief Secretary Wyndham and his Catholic Under-Secretary Sir Antony MacDonnell were unwilling to protect peaceful citizens; under Home Rule Protestants would be driven out like the Jews.[26]

Thus the Catholic Association and the Limerick boycott helped to stir up hardline Unionists against Wyndham and contributed to his downfall. Moran had no regrets. He regarded the idea that systematic nationalist co-operation with Wyndham might bring significant concessions as fantasy. The most prominent exponent of this view was William O'Brien, who resigned from the Irish Party and established a Cork-based dissident group.

Moran's emphasis on the alien nature of the Irish (especially the Ulster) Protestant had an unexpected by-product. In 1905 Arthur Clery began to advocate partition, and debated the subject with Eoin MacNeill. Clery was inspired partly by fear that a large Protestant minority allied with Catholic West Britons might maintain Protestant/Masonic influence in an autonomous Ireland, partly by distrust of urban Ulster Catholics, but his study of current affairs and his contacts with Ulster Unionists in the Law Library led him to see them as a distinct people entitled to remain within the United Kingdom by the same rights which entitled the rest of Ireland to secede from it. For the rest of his life Clery advocated partition with as few Catholics and Protestants as possible in the 'wrong' areas.[27] He is probably the only major nationalist intellectual who adopted a partitionist stance as a result of complete acceptance of the two-nation theory. This distinguishes him both from those like Father Michael O'Flanagan who advocated temporary acceptance of partition while hoping for eventual unity by consent, and those (like the later Moran) who accepted partition as unavoidable but hoped a powerful Gaelic and Catholic state would eventually absorb a weakened North.

One other point must be made. Despite Moran's denunciations of Protestants, he never advocated wholesale expulsion. *The Leader* was printed by Cahill's, a Protestant-owned firm. Moran said he employed Cahill's because they offered the best terms and recruited their employees fairly; he added that if they discriminated against Catholics, he would not use them on any terms.[28] Moran saw Protestants as resident aliens, and hoped they would be absorbed into Ireland, as he believed Irish emigrants would eventually be absorbed into Britain and America. Several mild Protestants, including the popular novelists Randall McDonnell and Lily MacManus, wrote for *The Leader*. Moran's attachment to free speech and love of controversy led him to admit more independent-minded Protestants, such as the separatist Alice Milligan, to his columns. He even published pieces by a few intrepid Unionists. The Rev. Dudley Fletcher, Rector of Portarlington, first appears in 1911 to give his views on the *Ne temere* decree and was still contributing occasionally in the late 1920s.

Moran was a bigot who helped to inflame existing religious bitterness; but it is important to see what sort of bigot he was. Because he had a sense of humour, a certain self-awareness, and some interest in the exchange of ideas for their own sake, he never quite reached the level of the hate-filled diatribes published by 'Sceilg' (J. J. O'Kelly) and Father Timothy Corcoran in the *Catholic Bulletin*.

Similarly, while there was a sectarian element in Moran's campaign against 'evil literature' and risqué plays, it was not purely sectarian. Moran acknowledged the role of Protestants in campaigning against 'evil literature' both in Ireland and in Britain. He attributed this to the fact that decent Protestants and Englishmen recognised obscenity when they saw it, whereas the Catholic Irish—despite hollow boasts about 'a land of saints and scholars'—were so cowardly that if a troop of devils came over from London, no-one would dare to protest, and the papers would praise the dignified and truly English manner in which they wagged their tails.[29] The solution, according to Moran, was renewed national self-confidence. Moran and his lieutenants poured scorn on the English culture which produced cheap papers, music-halls and the 'Rathmines Johnnies' who frequented them. Moran associated the Unionist *Irish Times* with this debased subculture by nicknaming it 'Alf Fox', the pseudonym of its horseracing tipster.[30] Sometimes, less subtly, he called it 'The Bigots' Dust Bin'. *The Leader* attacked risqué plays as 'The English Mind in Ireland'.

Moran knew that denunciations were not enough: Ireland must provide its own cheap popular entertainment. He saw the

24   D. P. MORAN

Gaelic League, with its meetings, concerts and dances, as an Irish Ireland alternative to the music-hall, and believed the League would destroy 'the English mind in Ireland' by reviving Irish and driving out English. Another short-term alternative was the Irish Literary Theatre.

Moran's relationship with the Irish Literary Theatre was always uneasy. In *The Philosophy of Irish Ireland* he denounced Yeats as a minor poet whose misty rhetoric concealed a shrewd business sense. Yeats, he said, marketed his verse in Britain as the authentic spirit of the Irish nation (which was far more Catholic and less superstitious than Yeats, and could only be expressed in Irish), then presented himself as a great Irish poet because of his English reputation, though most English people ignored his antics. There were very few great poets; Yeats was not one. The most anyone could hope to achieve was to be popular entertainer and instructor for their own generation; when Ireland was re-Gaelicised, her provincial writers would be forgotten.

Moran solicited a letter of welcome for the first issue of *The Leader* from Yeats, who replied ceremoniously. This was only a temporary suspension of hostilities. Moran continued to call Yeats a crypto-Protestant con-man. Ireland needed a Burns, not the pagan mystifications of a 'Saved' seer. For his part, Yeats thought Moran a dangerous philistine, without any intellectual tradition behind him, valuing only the obviously and immediately useful and whipping up popular prejudice.[31] Perhaps Moran's frustrated poetic ambitions fuelled his resentment against Yeats.

This tension marked Moran's early relations with the Irish Literary Theatre. George Moore cultivated Moran as a possible source of copy and even wrote for *The Leader* before it attacked his naturalistic play, *Diarmuid and Grania*. Thereafter Moran ridiculed 'Old Moore'; when Moore announced his conversion to Protestantism, *The Leader* hoped he would soon receive his soup and blankets.[32]

Moore once invited Moran and George Russell (AE), the theosophist poet and co-operative publicist, to dine. The guests took an instant dislike to each other, and the evening almost ended in blows. Moran nicknamed AE 'the Hairy Fairy' (the name spread rapidly through Dublin literary circles). AE thought Moran a tool of the Jesuits. Moran called AE 'a half-baked

A PLEA FOR ECONOMICS 25

Orangeman' (he was of Ulster Protestant origin). In 1904 AE wrote a pamphlet denouncing unnamed Dublin journalists for discourtesy in controversy; a fierce exchange ensued between AE and Moran.[33]

Moran's relations with Lady Gregory were more tranquil, though she shared Yeats's distrust of Moran; she occasionally wrote for *The Leader*, and offered to dramatise *Tom O'Kelly*.[34] Her farces and the satires of William Boyle were the only Abbey plays Moran enjoyed. He preferred the verse lampoons written by his contributor John Swift ('A.M.W.'), a gifted parodist who commented on current events in travesties of well-known ballads,[35] and sentimental light fiction, exemplified by the long-running *Leader* serial 'Our Ladies' Letter' (supposedly letters between Moll in the city and her sister Peg in the country, discussing household events and current politics).

Clery and Dawson, who wrote much of *The Leader's* early Abbey criticism, were more sophisticated but still fundamentally naïve. They expected the Abbey to create a 'folk-drama' ranking with Shakespeare or the Greeks; they had little understanding of the processes of artistic creation. They thought the achievements of the Abbey's early years were prentice pieces for the truly great work ahead. Dawson admired *Riders to the Sea*. Clery, like Moran, was disgusted by *Riders* but glad that after several near misses the Abbey had produced an undoubted masterpiece—Lady Gregory's *Kincora*.[36]

The only significant Abbey author closely involved with *The Leader* was Edward Martyn, who used it for a campaign to improve Irish church art. As by-products of Martyn's campaign, 'the gentle Ober' (Ober Meyer, a Munich stained-glass manufacturer) became one of Moran's regular targets, and Michael Healy, one of Sarah Purser's stained-glass artists, contributed cartoons to *The Leader*. Martyn became president of the Catholic Association, but when he also chaired Sinn Féin, Moran attacked him for linking the association with separatism.

The Playboy of the Western World finally drove a wedge between the Abbey and *The Leader*. Dawson, more sympathetic towards Synge than any other *Leader* critic, was sent to review the new play on its first night. Moran was surprised when Dawson produced a furious denunciation of the play, and went to see it out of curiosity. Moran's detestation was initially mitigated by dislike of the tactics of its opponents, but as the controversy developed *The Leader* hardened against *The Playboy*.[37] I know of no evidence to support the recent suggestion that Moran organised the *Playboy* riots.[38] Dislike of *The Playboy* was by no means confined to Moran. Griffith had compared Synge to the author of *Zaza* (a French play about a society prostitute), and *The Playboy* was denounced on patriotic grounds by Francis Sheehy Skeffington and his brother-in-law Francis Cruise O'Brien.[39]

The Leader still printed Abbey advertisements and reviewed productions, while abusing the company as 'the Pegeen Mikes'. When Yeats accepted a Civil List pension, *The Leader* depicted 'Constable Yeats, of the D.M.P. Arts Division' threatening to arrest Kathleen Ni Houlihan for causing a disturbance.[40]

Moran was reconciled with Martyn (who had broken with the Abbey) in 1910 after a ritual exchange of abuse, with Moran mocking Martyn's Sinn Féin activities and Martyn jeering at Moran's fantasies of political power. When Martyn died in 1923, Moran said 'he was too Irish for the West British crowd that exploited the Abbey'.[41]

Moran called Martyn's Sinn Féin allies childish 'tin-pikers'. When Griffith's 'Hungarian policy' was unveiled, he christened its proponents 'The Green Hungarian Band'. Moran compared Sinn Féin's appeal to the 1783 Renunciation Act to the Jacobitism of the eccentric Upper Thames Legitimist League. It was, he maintained, ridiculous to denounce the Act of Union as invalid *de jure* when it was unchallengeable *de facto*. Would 'King Edward VIII' (Martyn) or his successor as President of Sinn Féin, 'King John of Drumbaragh' (John Sweetman), refuse to pay 'illegal' income tax, see their furniture seized by 'unconstitutional' bailiffs, and be hauled by 'imaginary' policemen before a 'non-existent' law court?

Griffith reciprocated Moran's contempt. The Young Ireland writers were his ideological mentors; he disliked Moran's dismissal of Grattan and Davis as un-Irish. Griffith was puritanical, but saw Moran as too clericalist. (Griffith's papers got far fewer advertisements than *The Leader*.)[42] Above all, Griffith despised Moran's 'Collar the King' policy.

This policy was formulated when Edward VII visited Dublin in 1903. Moran argued that the traditional nationalist policy

A PLEA FOR ECONOMICS 27

(advocated by the Irish Party as well as by separatists) of shunning state occasions and refusing government appointments left the administration to Unionists and tame Catholics and allowed Unionists to dismiss Irish Party disavowals of separatism as insincere. He maintained that if Irish nationalists accepted autonomy within the Empire as the highest attainable measure of freedom, then they should be loyal to the crown as a constitutional symbol. Nationalists should demand their fair share of government jobs. Instead of boycotting the king or presenting abject addresses of loyalty, they should present a statement of grievances and offer loyalty if those grievances were removed. They should salute the Union Jack if it ceased to be a Unionist party flag, and sing 'God Save the King' when it no longer meant 'God Save the Anti-Idolator'.[43]

The 'Collar the King' policy is sometimes presented as a sign of increasing nationalist moderation. This ignores its sectarian undertones. It was first proposed when the Catholic Association was at its height, and it implied that the real enemy was not Britain but the Irish Protestant/Unionist community. Moran wanted nationalists to accept subordination to the Empire in external affairs in return for freedom to deal with the Protestants as they saw fit.

The 'Collar the King' policy was denounced by Griffith (in *The Resurrection of Hungary* 'jellyfish' advocate a similar policy)[44] and by Tom Kettle on behalf of the Irish Party.[45] None the less, after the Liberals returned to power in 1906 Moran claimed that the Irish Party was implementing his policy halfheartedly and without admitting it.

As the decade closed Moran drew closer to the Irish Party. The party is often seen as a monolithic bloc reflecting the attitudes of John Redmond. In fact it contained several factions; its members ranged from near-Unionists to virtual separatists. While most M.P.s and party activists took little interest in the new movements, some participated in Irish Ireland and industrial revivalist activities. Moran maintained contact with some younger party members such as Richard Hazleton (*Leader* contributor, University College graduate, member of the Young Ireland Branch of the U.I.L. and of Blackrock District Council, M.P. for North Galway after 1906) and John J. Horgan of Cork, who

28   D. P. MORAN

sometimes used the pen-name 'Pro Patria'. These were joined by
young intellectuals associated with the Young Ireland Branch,
formed among University College graduates to bring the party
into touch with new intellectual trends and to advocate a more
uncompromisingly nationalist policy. These Y.I.B.s (as they were
known) used *The Leader* to advocate greater freedom of debate
within the party, a rationalised party organisation, and a more
transparent and accountable leadership. The most prominent
were W. G. Fallon, Francis Cruise O'Brien, and the future Fianna
Fáil minister P. J. Little (Pádraig Mac Caoilte).

Relations between the Y.I.B. and *The Leader* were not always
harmonious. Some Y.I.B. stalwarts such as Kettle and the Sheehy
Skeffingtons detested *The Leader*, while Moran mocked the pretensions of the Y.I.B. Those Y.I.B.s who wrote for *The Leader* did not
necessarily endorse Moran's agenda; they took advantage of his
delight in clashing ideas to express their own viewpoints.[46]

Nevertheless, Moran thought the Irish Party was moving in his
direction. John Dillon still opposed compulsory Irish, but a U.I.L.
convention endorsed compulsory Irish for entrance to the new
National University. Redmond spoke of conciliating Protestants,
and T. P. O'Connor wrote for cheap English papers which
Moran excluded from his house; but the party was increasingly
influenced by the exclusively Catholic Ancient Order of
Hibernians, which formed its own patronage network and sought
jobs for Catholics as vigorously as the Catholic Association could
have desired. The A.O.H. was denounced by William O'Brien
(still pursuing, in his own eccentric way, a policy of conciliation
with Protestants); this merely served to recommend the organisation in Moran's eyes. Moran had by this time also tired of Healy's
maverick behaviour. (Healy was now allied with O'Brien.) The
antics of O'Brien, Healy and Griffith highlighted the advantages
of a single party; Redmond seemed statesmanlike by comparison.

The Irish Ireland agenda could not be attained by voluntary
action alone. Competitive examination on the railways had been
won through pressure at Westminster. Gaelic League membership
had levelled off;[47] success over compulsory Irish for the university
was partly due to political pressure. The industrial movement was
encountering setbacks; several prominent enterprises had failed.
Home Rule might give Irish Ireland state power; and by the

A PLEA FOR ECONOMICS 29

beginning of 1910 Home Rule seemed less remote than it had done when Moran founded *The Leader* and emphasised the difference between nationality and politics.

Before following Moran through the period of constitutional upheaval from January 1910 to the end of the Civil War in 1923, we shall glimpse at his domestic life. His whole life revolved around *The Leader*. He never took a holiday of any length, never revisited the Gaeltacht, and only once went abroad after the paper was founded. In the summer the Morans took a house by the seaside (usually Skerries), but Moran visited the office every day. He administered the paper from its city centre offices, but did his writing at home in the evenings. He liked to write in the room where Teresa was sewing, try his witticisms on her, and ask her opinion of articles. The house was littered with papers; the Moran children (four sons and a daughter, Nuala) were told not to throw away anything in case their father needed it. (The office was similarly cluttered; Moran cleared it by holocausts of superfluous documents, setting the chimney on fire.) The children were brought up on *Gill's Irish Reciter*, sent to Ring (the Waterford Gaeltacht) on holidays, and given an Irish Ireland education as far as possible. Father Dinneen came once a year for Christmas dinner; he gave the children presents, and they saw him as a Gaelic Santa Claus.[48]

The Morans held regular 'at homes'. These were important events for many contributors who were bachelors, timid, and often lonely. Clery was intellectually daring, physically brave, and recklessly outspoken on public platforms, but very shy in private. 'Imaal' (O'Toole) was outspoken in print but quiet in person; at the 'at homes' Moran often found him silently admiring Dawson's witty conversation.[49]

Even Moran was quieter and more good-humoured in private than in *The Leader*. He disliked speechmaking and rarely attended public meetings. He claimed to bear no ill-will against the people he attacked. This was often true (his children remembered being warned against grudges; his quarrels with Pearse did not keep him from promoting St Enda's), but the intensity of his attacks on Yeats, AE and (later) de Valera does suggest personal hostility. Perhaps for Moran, as for many contributors, the brash editorial voice of *The Leader* was a persona created to cope with a complex

30 D. P. MORAN

and threatening world and express hopes, fears, resentments and dreams excluded from everyday conversation.

Thus Moran exemplified the work-ethic he preached; but was this intermeshing of business and personal life as much a limitation as an asset? In 1906 or 1907 Moran could have raised the capital for a *Daily Leader*. He mentioned the idea occasionally but decided against it. Moran said he could not stand the discipline needed to run a paper of news rather than views, and decided he could not make it a financial success[50] (even though *The Leader* had established a strong brand-name). But perhaps *The Leader* also suffered from the characteristic flaw of family businesses— preference for security and continuing family control rather than a willingness to face the risks involved in expansion.

3

TWISTING THE SOURFACES, 1910–23

The reviving prospect of Home Rule did not lead Moran to neglect other causes. In 1911 he supported a new Crusade Against Evil Literature.[1]

Such campaigns had been mounted sporadically in Ireland since the 1880s, but this was more extensive than any predecessor. Inspired by a similar movement in England and by a lecture delivered to the Catholic Truth Society of Ireland by the English Catholic writer Canon William Barry, Vigilance Committees were established in the larger Irish towns (beginning in Limerick).

Newsagents selling 'immoral' newspapers were picketed; crowds met trains to seize and burn parcels of newspapers; music-hall performances were disrupted. The publishing firm of M. H. Gill & Co. founded the *Catholic Bulletin* as a guide to good reading (often items published by M. H. Gill & Co.).[2] Even Parnell's memory was invoked in this attempt to shake off English influence.[3] As the political temperature rose the Vigilance Committees died away (despite attempts by *The Leader* to revive them), and by 1918 they survived only in Dublin and Limerick; but they revived after the war and spearheaded the 1920s campaign which led to the Censorship of Publications Act.

The strongest opponent of the campaign was Francis Sheehy Skeffington, who attacked it as an assault on freedom and complained that it targeted religious heterodoxy. Moran denounced Sheehy Skeffington as a 'carrion sparrow' and demanded his expulsion from the Y.I.B. This was in fact an empty gesture, as Sheehy Skeffington resigned from the U.I.L. in protest at the failure of the Home Rule Bill to incorporate women's suffrage.[4]

Moran did not oppose female suffrage in principle; he believed that women property-holders should have the vote.[5] (Moran's belief in the primacy of economics over politics led him to favour a property qualification for all voters.) However, he

32 D. P. MORAN

believed that Home Rule should come first; female suffrage must wait if it endangered the bill. This view was widely shared. (It was expressed, for example, by Francis Cruise O'Brien in a *Leader* controversy with a suffragette, possibly Hanna Sheehy Skeffington.)[6] Suffragettes protested at the Dublin rally celebrating the introduction of the bill, and were attacked by A.O.H. stewards; suffragettes broke into U.I.L. headquarters; A.O.H. thugs disrupted a suffragette meeting in the Phoenix Park and chased participants into the zoo. *The Leader* celebrated with verses entitled 'Skeffy in the Zoo'. This rhyme enjoyed a wide circulation; street urchins sang it as Sheehy Skeffington passed.[7] Suffragette support for the Unionist candidate in the Londonderry City by-election in 1913 intensified hostility; at one point Moran said the suffragettes had converted him from women's suffrage.[8]

From 1912 *The Leader* published a weekly cartoon by Tom Lalor with verse commentary by 'A.M.W.'. Francis Sheehy Skeffington was a regular target. He appeared in the chimpanzees' tea-party at the zoo; as a monkey on the suffragette barrel-organ; as a sphinx saluted by the stereotypical suffragette (ugly, withered, demented and upper-class). Sheehy Skeffington took this abuse remarkably well; Moran said he enjoyed notoriety.[9]

The Leader was particularly vehement against Unionist opposition to Home Rule. After greeting the introduction of the bill with a cry of triumph (encouraged by increased circulation due to political excitement), Moran hinted that if the bill were defeated, nationalists should boycott Unionist businesses. Redmond warned nationalists to avoid bigotry; Moran retorted that the only bigotry in Ireland was anti-Catholic bigotry and that *The Leader* had always fought it.[10] Party speakers instanced cases where Nationalist local authorities appointed Protestants to vacancies. Moran promptly declared that they should be ashamed of themselves for pampering Protestants while Unionist authorities discriminated against Catholics. (In taking this line, Moran was supported by the *Catholic Bulletin.*)[11]

The Leader's Ulster correspondents—including the Belfast Gaelic Leaguer Father Richard Fullerton and 'Eirne' from Fermanagh (possibly Cahir Healy)—described Orange violence,

TWISTING THE SOURFACES, 1910–23 33

bigotry and anti-Catholic discrimination. They redoubled their activity after the Belfast riots of July 1913, when thousands of Catholics were driven from their workplaces. As refugees fled Belfast (some reaching Dublin) Moran published vivid accounts of sectarian brutality and supported attempts to organise a Belfast boycott.[12] He added that Southern Protestants shared responsibility for the behaviour of the 'Orange bolt-throwers' since most of them had not condemned it.

This embryonic Belfast boycott reflected another aspect of Moran's anti-Unionist campaign: denial that Ulster was more economically advanced than the rest of Ireland. He published articles by the statistician T. Galloway Rigg arguing that Ulster was less prosperous than Leinster and only slightly ahead of the other provinces. Rigg (who had advanced similar arguments in the debate on the Second Home Rule Bill)[13] followed with a long series based on the 1911 census, arguing that outside north-east Ulster the Protestant population (like the population in general) was decaying so rapidly under the Union that it couldn't possibly do worse under Home Rule. Other contributors denounced the Belfast economy as a 'bubble' based on weak-kneed Southern retailers buying from Northern wholesalers and Protestant banks lending the deposits of unenterprising Southerners at favourable terms to Protestant businessmen while charging Catholic entrepreneurs prohibitive rates. Sweated female labour in the Northern textile industry was emphasised. The Northern Protestant working class was presented as a race of idiots whose blind bigotry allowed their bloated oppressors to lead them by the nose. (Tom Lalor's cartoons portrayed 'Orange bolt-throwers' as muscle-bound anthropoids with tiny cloth-capped skulls.)

Moran's attitude to the growth of the Irish Transport and General Workers' Union was ambivalent. He had attacked 'the Irish striking man' as a danger to Irish industry, and *The Leader* regularly denounced trade societies and workingmen's clubs for favouring drink and other un-Irish pastimes. On the other hand, some contributors had social consciences; furthermore, the blatant poverty of the slums affronted Moran's love of efficiency, and dissatisfaction with the corrupt political machines and vested interests which dominated Dublin Corporation encouraged fellow-feeling for their labour opponents. (The price-raising activi-

34 D. P. MORAN

ties of Dublin traders affected Moran's white-collar readers as well as the slum-dwellers.) At first Moran extended sympathy to the I.T.G.W.U. They were an Irish union opposing English control; their principal opponent was the Chamber of Commerce, led by William Martin Murphy. (An I.T.G.W.U. activist, William Partridge, supplied Moran with information for his campaign against the railways.)[14] Moran contrasted the Unionist pronouncements of the *Irish Times* with its denunciations of English trade unionists meddling in Irish affairs.[15]

Moran was alienated by the sympathy strike (he said a dispute in a huckster's shop could shut down the whole country) and by Larkin's revolutionary rhetoric. (Moran maintained that Ireland needed more capitalists to exploit her.) His opposition to the 1913 strike was consolidated by the plan to take strikers' children to England. Moran had just begun one of his regular campaigns against Protestant proselytisers in the Dublin slums and saw the scheme as souperism in disguise; he joined the A.O.H.-organised mob which forcibly prevented the embarkation.[16] He held up the defeat of the strike as proof that English socialists were English first and socialists afterwards.

The Leader burlesqued the theatrical oratory of Carson and his lieutenants and portrayed the U.V.F. as a gaggle of schoolboys and greybeards with wooden guns. Moran called on the government to arrest the Ulster leaders; he occasionally spoke of basing a nationalist volunteer force on the A.O.H.[17] His views about how such a force might be employed were eccentric (he suggested that A.O.H. parades in Ulster should carry the Union Jack, so that an attack on a parade could be represented as an attack on the flag),[18] but he was invited to join the Irish Volunteers' Provisional Committee when it was formed in November 1913.

Moran declined this offer because he was too busy with his paper. This was his second 'great refusal'.[19] Since 1910 a few *Leader* contributors had fantasised about Moran entering politics as a second Parnell, the O'Connell of a new Catholic Association. Moran himself thought of a political career under Home Rule. Early in 1914 he announced his candidacy for the new Home Rule parliament.[20]

Such hopes would almost certainly have been disappointed. Moran was a poor speaker, and too independent to be a good

TWISTING THE SOURFACES, 1910–23 35

party man. A seat on the Volunteer Committee was not necessarily a passport to post-independence political success; Moran might have been compromised in its factional quarrels. (*The Leader* glorified the Volunteers but supported Redmond's demand for control because of the *Irish Times*'s attempts to sow dissension between the Irish Party and the Volunteers.) We shall never know how he would have fared as a public representative, for once again Moran preferred economics to politics.

Moran was still claiming that the Ulster agitation was all bluff long after its true dimensions were apparent. He said that the so-called 'Curragh mutiny' would make the government more determined to pass the Home Rule Bill; a fortnight after the Larne gun-running he still insisted that no guns had been landed.[21] He reacted angrily to government harassment of the Irish Volunteers, seen as favouritism towards the U.V.F. At his Abbey Street office, Moran heard the shots in Bachelor's Walk which followed the landing of Volunteer guns at Howth. His denunciations of the killings were so ferocious as to suggest that he thought them the first shots of civil war.[22]

Then war broke out in Europe. Moran was shocked by the war hysteria of the first days. He declared that Irishmen should stay at home, increase production, and guard Ireland's shores as Volunteers. (He once suggested that Ireland might spare 20,000 recruits, but quickly abandoned this position.) When Redmond called for recruits, *The Leader* broke with him.[23]

Moran's anti-recruiting stance surprised separatists,[24] but Moran had always been a 'Little Irelander'. He denounced Irish newspapers for carrying too much foreign news. Even during the Home Rule controversy Moran boasted that he ignored political events in Britain.[25] The 'Collar the King' policy had not foreseen a major war. Moran had assumed it could never happen because the expense would be ruinous to all the participants. His intellectual mentors were Little Englanders and pro-Boers; he knew the effect of the Boer War on the British budget and government stock. When it happened, Moran decided the demands of war on such a scale were too high a price for Home Rule.

The Leader did not identify itself with the Irish Volunteers under Eoin MacNeill (though Clery was a Volunteer and MacNeill wrote an article for *The Leader*). This may have been partly due to caution (several separatist papers were suppressed at the

36 D. P. MORAN

beginning of the war; the Special Branch kept *The Leader* under observation and warned its printer),[26] though *The Leader* continued to oppose recruiting, attack employers who put pressure on their workers to join up, and denounce government action against Volunteers and separatists. It even published pro-German articles by Galloway Rigg and Clery, though these were balanced by contributions from pro-Allied writers.

Moran was returning to *The Leader*'s traditional preoccupation with cultural and economic affairs, now the prospect of political triumph had receded. The most notable product of this cultural activism was a series by Piaras Béaslaí advocating an Irish-speaking league with a distinctive badge. This led to the formation of the Fáinne Gaelach.[27]

Moran serialised *The Philosophy of Irish Ireland* to recall its teachings for a new generation. He had been disturbed by the pro-British enthusiasm of August 1914. Clery was far more deeply affected; he lost faith in democracy and decided that liberalism was simply a façade used by selfish Masonic bourgeois elites to deceive the masses. He speculated that since the Irish had so readily abandoned their traditional hatred of Britain, their religion might be 'rushed' equally unexpectedly. A few months before the Easter Rising, Clery gloomily observed that the movement started by Hyde and Moran had spent its force; it would be 1925 before a new movement would arise to begin the last desperate struggle to preserve Irish nationality.[28]

Moran was concerned at the economic effects of the war. Wartime price rises affected his urban readers. *The Leader* was horrified by the speed with which farmers exported food in the autumn of 1914 in order to take advantage of the high prices at a time when the war was expected to be over by Christmas. From late 1914 Moran regularly predicted a new Famine; the urban poor were going hungry, and his readers might be next. Tom Lalor depicted farmers exporting all their produce and finding too late that they could not eat paper money.[29]

Throughout 1915 *The Leader* denounced farmers. They were accused of irrational antipathy to tillage, lack of economic enterprise, shortsighted profiteering, and depopulating the country by driving their children and labourers to emigrate in order to escape exploitation. (Several correspondents gave the farmers' viewpoint.)

TWISTING THE SOURFACES, 1910–23   37

In a short-sighted piece of war economy, the government suspended the Congested Districts Board's land reclamation and land division schemes and rented out its landholdings as pasture. This contradicted Department of Agriculture calls for tillage. Moran denounced 'the Congested Bullocks' Board' and published articles on the topic by Father Michael O'Flanagan. Moran denounced the arrest of separatists under emergency legislation. He attacked increased war taxation. He supported agitations by separatists and Irish Party dissidents against taxes and cutbacks. He told the party to become more independent of the government. He insisted that the war was bankrupting Britain and dragging Ireland down with her.[30]

As Moran went to his office on Easter Monday 1916 he saw the Volunteers in O'Connell Street. He went home as the shooting began. His office, with all *The Leader*'s records, was destroyed in the fighting.

Moran secured a new office and resumed publication after three weeks' incessant work. The paper immediately joined the debate over the attempted settlement offering immediate Home Rule with six counties excluded. With most separatist leaders dead or imprisoned, nationalist opposition in Ireland to the proposed settlement was led by Moran's old enemies Murphy, O'Brien and Healy and some Ulster nationalists. Moran supported the scheme; Lalor depicted Murphy and his allies dancing ring-o'-roses with Southern Unionists and Tory diehards. The issue was argued vigorously in *The Leader*, with 'Imaal' and Father O'Flanagan supporting the scheme for immediate Home Rule with partition, while 'Eirne' and Louis J. Walsh opposed it. Their debate continued after the collapse of the settlement.[31]

There seemed no serious alternative to the Irish Parliamentary Party. Moran supported Count Plunkett in the North Roscommon by-election, but questioned the creation of a new organisation. Since the Irish Party still seemed to have significant support, the appearance of a rival nationalist body might return the country to the political chaos of the 1890s, and another period of Unionist rule and soul-sapping Anglicisation might finally destroy Irish nationality. Moran therefore advised his readers to reform the party from within. He was encouraged by the fact that the party candidate in the South Longford by-election, the bacon producer

38 D. P. MORAN

Patrick McKenna, was a longstanding *Leader* subscriber and industrial revivalist.[32]

At first Moran thought the Sinn Féin victory in South Longford too narrow to be decisive; but as the prisoners interned after the rising returned to a heroes' welcome, as Irish Party support collapsed in East Clare, as the separatist groups united under de Valera, Moran realised that Sinn Féin was strong enough to dominate nationalist Ireland. He then told the old party to withdraw for the sake of national unity and proclaimed Sinn Féin heirs of the Irish Ireland movement. Contributors associated with the party had gone over to Sinn Féin or broken with *The Leader.* Only 'Imaal' supported the party to the end, and he did not express his views in *The Leader.*[33]

Moran declared that, if the Irish people (by which he meant the nationalists) could stay united, freedom must ultimately be gained, since Britain would be severely weakened at the end of the war. He saw the achievement of the Irish Ireland project at hand. The only major check to his hopes came when the Irish Party's three by-election wins in early 1918 indicated that it might survive as a rival to Sinn Féin. Clery attacked the Ulster Nationalists for opposing Sinn Féin as they opposed Parnell in 1891. 'They have taken Carson to their bosom. Let him take them to his bosom!'[34] Louis Walsh defended them; yet another debate on partition followed.

The conscription crisis of 1918 ended any prospect of an Irish Party revival. Moran exulted in the great upsurge of patriotic and religious feeling (adding that, with a few exceptions, Protestants supported conscription). Since the Gael held the land, he was bound to win in the end. He ridiculed rumours of a new land confiscation and plantation; the British were no longer strong enough. His only regret was that, with the loss of Irish Party influence over the government, civil service appointments were again a happy hunting-ground for Freemasons. The 1916 rising had damaged the paper commercially, but a contract with his paper supplier signed shortly before the outbreak of war enabled Moran to keep *The Leader* at its pre-war price of a penny until early 1918.[35] In the 1918 election Moran voted for Sinn Féin and jeered as the old party was swept aside.

Moran welcomed the new Dáil Éireann and rejoiced that its first meeting was conducted entirely in Irish. He attacked

TWISTING THE SOURFACES, 1910–23   39

attempts by moderate Unionists and Redmondites to establish a new centre party advocating a dominion settlement. Moran was not a doctrinaire republican; he simply feared that unauthorised programmes would weaken the Dáil.

Since 1916 Irish publications were subject to censorship. This had not seriously hindered Moran, but as separatist and Irish Ireland organisations were suppressed, and as killings began and repression increased, *The Leader* faced trouble. Moran wrote with conscious recklessness, expecting (almost hoping) to be suppressed.[36] The blow fell because of a Dáil loan advertisement published in August 1919. All papers carrying it were suppressed. Publication could only resume if the proprietor agreed not to publish such material again. The proprietors refused. Nuala Moran was just beginning to publish articles (as 'Niamh'). Many years later she recalled how, while her father tried to look cheerful, his world seemed to collapse.[37]

Six weeks later the *New Leader* appeared. Moran persuaded the veteran Irish Irelander Joseph Dolan of Ardee to register as nominal proprietor. This required complete mutual trust. Dolan could have claimed the paper as his property. Moran could have referred creditors to Dolan (who had already lost a lot of money through loans to Pearse). Dolan could have been imprisoned if the government decided that Moran was publishing sedition. Moran revived the title *The Leader* in mid-1920, acting in the assumption that Dublin Castle was too busy with the I.R.A. to notice.[38] For the rest of his life he praised Dolan's generosity.

Business considerations also dictated prudence. *The Leader* had suffered severe financial loss through the break in publication. (Nuala believed the paper never fully recovered from the setbacks of 1916 and 1919.) Some of its most committed contributors were otherwise occupied. Walsh was in prison. Clery, one of the few barristers willing to become a Sinn Féin judge, was now a member of the Supreme Court of the Republic.[39]

Hence, while Moran still denounced the British government and Dublin Castle, he made only guarded references to the activities of the I.R.A. and crown forces. He said the newspapers were so like a morgue or a chamber of horrors that he could not bear to review their contents.

40 D. P. MORAN

The end of the war brought many business mergers, with small Irish-owned firms swallowed by British rivals; Moran urged readers to boycott firms which gave up their independence. For a time he praised attempts at co-operative production, which would ensure Irish control. He criticised vast schemes for neo-Gaelic co-operative commonwealths but favoured small-scale experiments. The Dublin Co-operative Wholesale Clothing Company, managed by the Labour publicist and former *Leader* contributor L. P. Byrne, attracted Moran's praise; but Irish workers ignored the co-operatives established for their benefit.

Moran told farmers to invest war profits in Irish industries. He denounced the new Farmers' Unions for their social pretensions and foreign dances on festive occasions. While *The Leader* criticised both sides in the farm labourers' strikes, it favoured the labourers.

Moran's denunciation of the farmers' dances reflected a wider phenomenon. The moralist crusades of the 1920s are sometimes seen as a reaction to the Civil War. They were in fact a reaction to social changes caused by the First World War. In 1919 the vigilance associations revived. Professor Magennis, the future censor, orated in the Rotunda about immoral films (a frequent *Leader* theme). Moran complained that cheap English papers were not merely immoral but anti-Irish; yet they sold widely in Dublin. *The Leader* thundered against new fashions in women's dress as lewd, un-Irish and unpatriotic, since Irish manufacturers had ignored the new trends. (Lalor would not draw a woman wearing these immoral garments; he showed a shop assistant holding a sleeveless dress, hem midway between knee and ankle.)[40] Moran denounced the 'bona-fide travellers' who passed his house to get drunk in Finglas, and called 'Mr Bung', his archetypal publican, 'Britain's greatest tax collector'.

Large-scale riots and pogroms in the North from 1920 were highlighted as proof of Orange savagery. When a new Belfast boycott (beginning, as in 1913, in Tuam) was adopted by the Dáil, Moran said that events would have been very different had Tuam been heeded in 1913. He declared the Northern economy could not withstand a boycott; the economic depression in Britain and extensive government cutbacks (the 'Geddes axe') showed that Britain could not afford Ireland and must hand it over—Orangemen included—to Sinn Féin.[41]

TWISTING THE SOURFACES, 1910–23   41

Moran saw the truce of July 1921 as proof of his analysis.[42] He praised the I.R.A. and its leaders. He delighted in the rush to the language classes as enthusiasts and opportunists prepared for the new regime; he painted a pleasant, selective picture of the South relaxing with Irish textbooks while the North sank into anarchy. Moran predicted a bright future of cultural revival and business confidence after a settlement.

Moran was satisfied with the Treaty. It gave more than he (or most of the Irish population) had expected to see in his lifetime. He was particularly impressed by the cession of fiscal autonomy. The oath was a formality, the king was a rubber stamp; both were acceptable under protest. Partition was regrettable, but a side issue.

Clery, the partitionist, was the only major *Leader* contributor to oppose the Treaty. He predicted dire consequences, though when challenged to explain what alternative there was, he retreated into evasion and flippancy. He saw the Treaty's oath of allegiance, instinctively and beyond debate, as 'the Devil's Sacrament', a renunciation of faith; once it was accepted, everything else would ultimately be lost.[43] Clery sacrificed the chance of high judicial office and refused a pension of £400 a year rather than recognise the Free State. He added to his sacrifices by observing the convention that former judges do not practise at the bar.

Moran could not understand the Republicans. He was depressed by the low intellectual level of the Treaty debates, the personal abuse and the fact that they were conducted in English. (Clery remarked gloomily that this showed the shallowness of the Gaelic revival.)

When the Dáil approved the Treaty, Moran asked the factions to settle down as a civilised government and opposition. He reminded them of the squabbles which discredited the old Irish Party. Moran had paid so much attention to the crimes of the British and Orangemen, and so little to the I.R.A., that he forgot the potential violence of private armies. Not until de Valera spoke of 'wading through Irish blood' did Moran realise that this was incipient civil war. [44]

Moran pleaded for peace. He pointed to the loss of Gaelic enthusiasm, the collapse of business confidence, the paralysis of trade.[45] Lalor portrayed Carson and Orangemen jeering at the quarrel while world opinion stood bewildered.

When fighting broke out, Moran first hoped it would end in Dublin, then with the fall of the Republican strongholds in Munster. *The Leader* publicised wanton violence and destruction by Republicans trying to make the country ungovernable. At every disaster Moran told his readers to keep up their spirits.

Early in 1923 Moran said he could pretend no longer. The Irish people, given a unique opportunity, had squandered it. The only beneficiaries were Unionists and Freemasons. There would probably be another plantation; Irish stupidity deserved it.[46]

4

THE PHILOSOPHY OF INDEPENDENT IRELAND, 1923–36

Moran's despair did not last. He found a new source of hope: tariffs. He was neither a doctrinaire free-trader nor a doctrinaire protectionist. At first he thought the new state should avoid tariffs because they encouraged complacency and vested interests. But the Civil War had shaken his confidence that the Irish economy could revive without substantial encouragement. His conversion to protection was completed by the discovery that even Britain, that noted exponent of free trade, found certain tariffs necessary.[1]

A protectionist lobby emerged among supporters of the Free State government. It centred on the Cork and Dublin I.D.A.s (later merged in the protectionist National Agricultural and Industrial Development Association—N.A.I.D.A.). Leading spokesmen were Cork businessmen Andrew O'Shaughnessy (now a T.D.), the Dowdall brothers (both became senators), and veteran Sinn Féiners William Sears, T.D., and Senator James McKean. J. J. Walsh, the Postmaster-General, spoke for protectionism in the cabinet.[2]

Moran was linked to the Cork group (though he thought Walsh incompetent). *The Leader* became their principal press mouthpiece and regularly published statements by businessmen thanking Moran for his vigorous advocacy of protection. Moran also backed other pro-business measures, such as a campaign by another Cork businessman, Hugo Flinn, to remit income tax on profits from Irish-owned industries. (Flinn later became a Fianna Fáil junior minister.)[3]

Not all businessmen supported protection. The distributing trades and Chambers of Commerce opposed it. Goulding had died; Moran's new choice as symbol of the political and economic enemy was David Barry, chairman of the B&I shipping line (with a vested interest in extensive Anglo-Irish trade). When de Valera was arrested in Northern Ireland, Moran wanted Barry seized and held as a hostage by the Free State government.[4]

44   D. P. MORAN

Moran sneered when told that tariffs would copperfasten partition. He praised partition as a blessing in disguise. If the North had come in, there would have been a much larger pro-British element; compulsory Irish might not have been introduced, and it would have been much harder to ban divorce, tighten censorship and impose tariffs. Tariff-protected industries would have gravitated to the industrialised Belfast region and employed Orangemen or British immigrants; instead Northern firms were opening branches in the South.[5]

He saw the decline of the great exporting industries of the North, and gloated that in a generation the impoverished North would come begging to a booming South to get in on any terms. Moran hoped that as many Orangemen as possible would emigrate before the rest surrendered to the Saorstát complete with tariffs, censorship and compulsory Irish.[6] The Boundary Commission was disappointing, but Moran had not expected much. His correspondents (including Clery) had predicted failure for some time. Clery suggested the commission's chairman, Mr Justice Feetham, would be remembered as 'Mr Justice Cheat'em'.[7]

Protectionism had moral overtones. One contributor linked 'free thought, free trade and free literature' as English plagues.[8] Moran regularly demanded a tariff on English newspapers which, he claimed, were corrupting Irish morals and undercutting Irish newspapers through economies of scale. *The Leader* praised groups such as the Angelic Warfare Association of St Thomas Aquinas, a Cork-based sodality which organised Gaeltacht camps for young men and seized and destroyed foreign newspapers.[9] Opposition to the Free State coinage designs, voiced by Moran himself and contributors such as the young Leon Ó Broin, insisted that the new designs were pagan and Protestant because of the involvement of Yeats and the absence of any religious symbols, and the presentation of farm animals as symbols of the nation's wealth was seen as reflecting the pro-grazier, free-trade economic policy of the Chambers of Commerce and the Minister for Agriculture, Patrick Hogan.[10]

The politico-cultural debates of the 1920s are sometimes presented as a conflict between the *Irish Statesman* and the *Catholic Bulletin*.[11] This is an illusion created by the *Bulletin*'s obsession

THE PHILOSOPHY OF INDEPENDENT IRELAND, 1923–36   45

with the *Statesman*. Moran often attacked 'the hairy fairies and their Plunkett House paper' for their advocacy of free trade and opposition to censorship and compulsory Irish, but he saw the *Irish Times* as his main ex-Unionist adversary. David Barry attracted more of his attention than Yeats (though *The Leader* attacked the appointment of 'this minor West British poet' to the Senate, and commented on his divorce speech: 'Mr Yeats has divorced Kathleen Ni Houlihan and formed an alliance with Dolly Brae').[12]

Moran regularly denounced 'Union Jackasses' who sang 'God Save the King' at the Dublin Horse Show and 'Poppyites' who congregated on Armistice Day. He complained about the ex-Unionist presence in the Senate and stood against an ex-Unionist in a co-option contest in February 1926. (Moran was proposed by the protectionist Senator McKean and was defeated by 40 votes to 10 in a secret ballot.)[13] He did not, however, see ex-Unionists as the only, or even the main, enemy; he called them a defeated remnant doomed to absorption. Moran noted with satisfaction the *Irish Times*'s lament that most Protestant leaders and elected representatives were silent on unpalatable legislation.[14]

The other great enemy was the Catholic 'West Briton'. The *Irish Independent*, which supported free trade, was as unpalatable as the *Irish Times*. The Farmers' Union and its associated Farmers' Party were dominated by larger farmers who wanted to continue selling live cattle to Britain and importing cheap manufactured goods. (This was the policy of Hogan and the five-member Fiscal Inquiry Committee of economists.) The Farmers' Union disliked the government decision to make Irish compulsory for many jobs and force all schools to teach Irish; some farmer leaders, such as the east Cork ex-Redmondite D. L. O'Gorman, explicitly opposed it.[15]

Moran respected Hogan's energy and ability, but called him 'the Minister for Grass and Emigration'. The 'Fiscal Five' were denounced as typical academics, divorced from the real world. Their 'Green Grass for a Green People' would reduce Ireland to '200,000 ranchers, herds and hucksters'.

Moran's view of farmers was summed up in a notorious cartoon. An obese farmer basks in a grassy plain containing one house, a few trees and several bullocks. Inset pictures show hordes of officials at the Department for Educating Farmers and a

46 D. P. MORAN

taxpayer carrying a burden marked 'Land Purchase'. The farmer remarks: 'Irish manufacturers are very inefficient!'[16]

This aroused a storm of protest from farmer correspondents. Moran's city-boy errors were pointed out. He spoke as if bullocks rained fully-grown from the sky; he was reminded that considerable care was needed to bring them to marketable condition.

Moran's advocacy of protection did not stifle his commitment to free debate. Two contributors regularly put the case for free trade.[17] Some contributors (notably John Sweetman, the octogenarian former President of Sinn Féin) wanted total self-sufficiency, but Moran insisted that protection could only be a temporary expedient and might easily create exploitative monopolies and economic stagnation (as in America).

Now that independence was secure, Moran spoke of relaxing a few restrictions. He told ultra-purist Gaelic musicians they must adapt or be left behind 'worshipping the bones of their ancestors . . . some of the bones are of doubtful authenticity'. He attacked the G.A.A. ban and praised the Irish rugby team as a focus of national identity. This horrified Clery, who saw the popularity of rugby as a. symptom of post-Treaty demoralisation, leading inexorably to a new Union.[18]

For Moran this encapsulated what was wrong with the Republicans and the Irish people as a whole. They did not realise they were free to use their new powers. He spoke of writing a new book, to be entitled 'The Philosophy of Independent Ireland.' Moran sometimes praised particular statements or proposals by Republicans, but said that until they realised Ireland was free they were as irrelevant as the Upper Thames Legitimist League. (Clery still admired Moran and praised him for publishing Republican views suppressed by the mainstream press; Moran, for his part, called Clery's pessimism a valuable stimulant.)

Despite regular editorial grumblings about Masonic influence, Moran attacked those who claimed the whole country was run by Freemasons. Since Ireland was now free, the Freemasons were an insignificant minority; if they were clever enough to control the country, it served the 'mere Irish' right for incompetence. Moran described the gravitation of ex-Unionists to Cumann na nGaedheal as proof that absorption had begun. He attributed the shortcomings of Cumann na nGaedheal to sincere mistakes rather than any

THE PHILOSOPHY OF INDEPENDENT IRELAND, 1923–36   47

occult influence; he pointed out that they had made no concessions to Protestants on compulsory Irish and praised them for tightening licensing laws and for the Shannon scheme.[19]

In 1926, when the *Irish Independent*, supported by the Farmers' Party and the neo-Redmondite National League, attacked the Cosgrave government as wasteful, Moran defended Cumann na nGaedheal. He said they had done as well as could be expected, given the world depression and war damage. The civil service gave value for money. (Many readers were civil servants; 'Imaal's' final article defended the civil service.)[20] Wage cuts merely reduced consumer demand. Protectionism would increase government revenue, avoid state meddling with individual enterprises, and extend the home market by increasing purchasing power.

Moran favoured reflation, but was unsure how it could be done. He allowed advocates of the Social Credit scheme of Major Douglas to write extensively in *The Leader*—even though he believed their scheme would create uncontrollable inflation—because he thought debate about their ideas would educate the public on currency and credit. Moran wanted an independent Irish currency eventually, but opposed 'handing over the printing press to the great statesmen on our back benches' until the public were better educated.[21]

Keynes's economic writings are cited occasionally in *The Leader* in the late 1920s. The Douglasites quoted him on money in support of their attacks on bankers; Sweetman cited him on overproduction as 'proof' that under modern methods of production a small nation can only survive by total autarky. Moran preferred the other leading British reflationist, Reginald McKenna. When Keynes visited Dublin in April 1933, Moran missed his lecture through pressure of work. When he read Keynes's lecture (with its numerous admissions of uncertainty), Moran jeered at him as a typical academic unable to handle the real world.[22]

In the political turbulence after the Boundary Commission and the secession of de Valera and his followers from Sinn Féin to found Fianna Fáil, Moran hoped for a political realignment and a strong protectionist Irish Ireland government, combining most of Cumann na nGaedheal and the moderate Republicans, facing a weak West British free-trade opposition formed from the Farmers' Party, ex-Unionists, the right wing of Cumann na nGaedheal, and the National League.[23]

48 D. P. MORAN

This assumed both that Republican extremists had enough support to prevent de Valera from forming a government on his own, and that the Cumann na nGaedheal protectionists would dominate their party. Instead Fianna Fáil became an alternative government, while the leading Cumann na nGaedheal protectionists were defeated.

Moran reluctantly endorsed Cumann na nGaedheal at both 1927 elections. When Fianna Fáil produced a protectionist economic programme in 1928, Moran endorsed de Valera's party. He said he supported measures, not men, and Fianna Fáil were now 'ex-anti-Treatyites', prepared to work the Treaty even if they were not prepared to admit it. He pointed to their recruitment of Hugo Flinn (Fianna Fáil T.D. for Cork City from 1927). Moran hoped Flinn would become Minister for Finance. Several of Moran's pro-Treaty associates now supported Fianna Fáil, notably the Dowdall brothers and John Sweetman. Moran also published articles by the erratic Patrick Belton calling for a protectionist farmers' organisation and an independent Irish currency.

Moran's sensitivity to the economic situation was influenced by the decline of *The Leader*. Many old targets had vanished; old issues and slogans had lost their potency. The nucleus of contributors was breaking up. 'A.M.W.' died in 1923. 'Imaal' followed in 1927. Rigg died in 1928.[24] Dinneen stopped writing for *The Leader* after he was disabled by an accident, and died in 1934.[25]

In November 1932 Arthur Clery died. De Valera's entry into the Dáil had deepened his gloom. Clery became Independent Republican T.D. for the National University in June 1927, but retired rather than take the oath of allegiance. He kept contact with both Fianna Fáil and Sinn Féin (he was one of de Valera's legal advisers on the land annuities), but predicted that Fianna Fáil would follow Cumann na nGaedheal. 'Austin Stack died, as he had lived, an Irishman,' wrote Clery. 'Most Irishmen of the middle classes die as Englishmen.'[26] He wondered whether his ascetic political and personal life had been worthwhile, but did not see how he could have done otherwise. He consoled himself with thoughts of the life to come, the new national movement he expected to arise about twenty years hence in what he predicted would be the dying Ireland of 1948, and some future Catholic statesman who would purify and reconcile the systems of Lenin

THE PHILOSOPHY OF INDEPENDENT IRELAND, 1923–36   49

and Mussolini and re-establish Catholicism and social justice from Moscow to Gibraltar.[27] William Dawson memorialised his cousin in several articles before his own death in 1934.[28]

Moran was ageing, his children were growing up. In 1928 the Morans moved from south Dublin to Skerries. In 1929 their two eldest sons died within a few months. The first death, in January, passed unmentioned in *The Leader*; in April a brief note explained that the editor believed he should not intrude his private life upon his readers and apologised for the curtailment of editorial notes due to the second death.[29]

Of the surviving children, Nuala (now employed in the Department of Education) took most interest in *The Leader*. She wrote a column about social and cultural events, signed 'N'. This was part of a tendency towards greater coverage of such matters.

Moran turned against Fianna Fáil in 1931. He detested de Valera's convoluted and selective self-justifications, his refusal to admit any mistake in his attitude towards the Treaty, his view of poverty as the price of freedom.[30] Fianna Fáil's refusal to admit the full legitimacy of the government or to disavow the I.R.A. reawakened fears which had not completely died. Moran briefly talked of supporting Labour if they would adopt protection; but the small Labour Party had no chance of power.

Moran moved reluctantly back to Cumann na nGaedheal because 'even Hogan's Grass is better than bloody grass'. His return cannot have been of much help to the government; several vociferous contributors continued to support Fianna Fáil, while Moran regularly lamented the slowness of progress towards tariffs and censorship. He complained that Hogan seemed to be the only cabinet minister who knew what he believed. Moran denounced Cumann na nGaedheal protectionists as cowardly slaves of the party whip. Repeated warnings that Irish tariffs would bring retaliation on the cattle trade provoked derision. Ministers' social pretensions aroused scorn.

The government's foreign policy achievements meant little to Moran. He praised the Statute of Westminster as a vindication of the Treaty, but thought ministers too concerned with international conferences. Rumours that the government might end partition or join a United States of Europe filled Moran with horror. He said a United States of Europe could never exist

50   D. P. MORAN

because countries would never give up control of their economies ('Nationality is too big a thing').[31]

In 1932 Moran hesitated until the last moment before endorsing Cumann na nGaedheal, and after the election he was glad Fianna Fáil had been given a chance. He predicted that they would last a few years (long enough to preclude any return to 'Hogan's Grass'), then break up in a new realignment.[32]

At first Moran was exhilarated by the speed with which new tariffs (including the long-awaited tariff on imported newspapers) were imposed; then he grew alarmed at the government's haste and recklessness. When de Valera, immediately after a long state visit to the continent, announced he would take no holiday that year, Moran denounced this insult to the intelligence of the Irish people. I.R.A. activity increased. Worst of all was the Economic War, for which Moran held de Valera entirely responsible. He pointed out that while the *Irish Press* (ironically called 'Truth in the News') was claiming that the British market no longer existed, de Valera paid a 10 per cent subsidy (funded by tax increases) to allow Irish cattle to compete in it. Moran compared this to 'feeding a dog with bits of his own tail' and 'waging war against ourselves, selling arms to the enemy and paying for the ammunition'.[33]

Moran opposed Fianna Fáil in 1933 more vigorously than in 1932, but pro-Fianna Fáil articles still appeared in *The Leader*, and after the election Moran again argued that Fianna Fáil deserved a fair trial. This courtesy soon vanished. After the dismissal of General O'Duffy as Police Commissioner, Moran attacked de Valera as a dictator and said his petty tyranny had inadvertently brought his destined successor into the political arena. 'O'Duffy is the word, and O'Duffy is the man!' Pro-Fianna Fáil contributors lay low, except Sweetman, who denounced de Valera's opponents as imperialists, the Blueshirts as fascists, and O'Duffy as an Irish Hitler.[34]

Had Moran become a fascist? He said that while de Valera had a majority of votes, the majority of sensible people who kept the country going had voted against Fianna Fáil; but Moran had long lamented the enfranchisement of 'boys and girls of 21', while recognising that nothing could be done about it.[35] He questioned whether de Valera's majority of one (supplemented by Labour support) was sufficient mandate for his actions; and given the

THE PHILOSOPHY OF INDEPENDENT IRELAND, 1923–36   51

sweeping changes involved and the absence of constitutional restraint, this view was not unreasonable.[36]

In the 1920s Moran occasionally referred to .Mussolini as a strong and effective ruler, but added that dictatorship would not suit the Free State. (Moran told the Blueshirts to stop wearing their uniforms because they imitated foreign movements.)[37] Moran also disapproved of Mussolini's jingoism. In 1935 he denounced Italian gloating over the slaughter of Abyssinian 'husbands, fathers, sons' as unchristian.[38] This attitude sprang from hatred of war rather than fondness for blacks (whom he habitually called 'niggers'). Moran's awareness of the human cost of war was related to his awareness of its economic cost. He was a pro-business conservative, not a fascist.

O'Duffy was widely seen as a distinguished public servant victimised by political opponents. Moran had never met O'Duffy personally and did not realise that he was a fascist. *The Leader* insisted that O'Duffy was a constitutional opposition leader because the General had promised to implement his corporatist programme by democratic means. Moran thought the programme too doctrinaire and suggested that it should be implemented piecemeal to see if it worked, but his Little Irelandism blinded him to the fact that it was inherently anti-democratic.[39] (This was obvious to some pro-Fine Gael contributors, who pointed out that it excluded opposition and required state regimentation of society and intervention in the family—practices incompatible with Catholic social teaching.)[40]

Moran believed 'Dictator de Valera' could not tolerate legitimate opposition. As he saw it, ten years earlier de Valera had plunged the country into civil war; now he tolerated I.R.A. activity and recruited a new Army Reserve from I.R.A. men. Members of the new force spoke from Fianna Fáil platforms and marched in uniform in Fianna Fáil processions; Moran thought Fianna Fáil was recruiting a private army.[41] (In fact it was buying off Republican opponents.) De Valera responded to calls for police protection of opposition meetings by saying it was not his business to protect opponents against their own unpopularity. Moran called this incitement, and pointed out that Blueshirts did not attack Fianna Fáil rallies.[42] When de Valera prohibited O'Duffy's march to Leinster House and moved police and troops into Dublin to prevent any coup attempt, Moran thought de Valera

52 D. P. MORAN

was planning a coup himself.[43] He expressed similar fears when de Valera accused opponents of wanting to overthrow the government by force; at times Moran apparently feared arrest.[44]

Moran hoped an upsurge of anti-government feeling would produce Fianna Fáil defections and topple de Valera—a hope dispelled by the 1934 local elections.[45] He welcomed Fine Gael's announcement of its conversion to tariffs and the promotion of Belton to its front bench. *The Leader* criticised the militaristic behaviour of the Blueshirts and their increased use of violence and illegality, but Moran was startled by the resignations of O'Duffy and Belton. Moran sided with the party.[46]

The situation relaxed as de Valera turned against the I.R.A. and concluded the Coal–Cattle Pact. Moran praised Cosgrave but admitted that Fine Gael was unlikely to form a government in the near future. He fantasised about a Fianna Fáil split and a Cosgrave-led national government. He named three Fianna Fáil ministers as indispensable: Tom Derrig, Minister for Education (for his commitment to Irish in schools), Seán T. O'Kelly (for his ebullient personality and his successful housing programme), and Seán Lemass, whose energy, enthusiasm and commitment to industrialisation commanded Moran's admiration.[47]

On 1 February 1936 D. P. Moran was suddenly taken ill as he prepared for work; a few hours later he died. The Dublin press (even the *Irish Times*) paid tribute. Fine Gael forgot the jeers at 'Hogan's Grass' and praised Moran as a self-sacrificing nation-builder. The funeral at Kilbarrack was attended by Cosgrave and several ex-ministers. Hugo Flinn represented Fianna Fáil. Louis Walsh and many old associates attended.[48]

Nuala Moran inherited the editorial chair. The paper gradually became less combative and more intellectual, with more social and cultural material (including the profiles which caused a famous libel suit by Patrick Kavanagh).[49] In the late 1940s it became a fortnightly and for some years experienced a second spring, renewed its links with U.C.D. and published high-quality comment by academics (notably T. Desmond Williams).[50] It remained staunchly Catholic (Nuala was active in the Legion of Mary) and regularly recalled its own history and the lifework of D. P. Moran. It went into decline in the 1960s, became a monthly, and ceased publication in 1971.

CONCLUSION

Conor Cruise O'Brien, the most recent analyst of Moran, sees him as the dark genius of Catholic nationalism: the Mephistopheles who blighted the Irish revival and brought Parnellite Dublin under the yoke of the Catholic Church.[1] This gives Moran a stature he did not achieve. He never attained the press baron status or the political leadership which some friends thought to be within his grasp. Yet he was indeed a dark genius; it is possible to see why great things were expected of him. He was a brilliant journalist and a talented entrepreneur. It is often assumed that Griffith represented the rising Catholic entrepreneurial class who would benefit from the tariffs he advocated. This interpretation forgets that before 1917 Griffith seemed unlikely ever to be in a position to implement tariffs, while lobbying Westminster brought real though limited benefits. In so far as the nationalist entrepreneurs had a spokesman, it was Moran.

Moran was an innovator, but also an exponent of a nationalist tradition, as old as O'Connell, of using abuse and ridicule to dispel deference and awaken the courage of the downtrodden.[2] The Parnellite tradition was more complex than is often realised; Parnell's experience in 1890–91 overshadows the political advantages Parnellites gained in the 1880s in pouring similar abuse on landlords and the Dublin Castle administration. *The Leader's* denunciations of 'tolerance proving' are a debased form of Parnell's contempt for those who sought to propitiate English opinion. Moran and several of his contributors had been Parnellites; his fights with Yeats can be seen as a struggle between rival claimants to the Chief's mantle.

Similarly, Moran did not poison with intolerance an originally untainted Gaelic League. The League was a populist movement exalting the wisdom of the folk; it defined itself against English mass culture. Hyde's *Necessity for De-Anglicising Ireland* contains many themes of *The Philosophy of Irish Ireland*: it was Hyde who first spoke of the English mind in Ireland.[3] The Gaelic League can be

53

portrayed as *potentially* pluralist, but it rapidly went from demanding fair treatment for Irish-speakers and teaching Irish to volunteers, to advocating the forcible repression of Anglo-Irish culture as Gaelic culture had formerly been repressed.

While the League as a whole, and its most prominent leaders, did not share Moran's sectarianism, it engaged in other forms of intolerance.[4] Neither Hyde nor MacNeill was prepared to acknowledge Anglo-Irish culture as legitimate. Hyde's background was almost as remote from metropolitan Unionism as those of Moran and MacNeill. He was the product of a dying provincial Toryism distant from the English mainstream and in everyday contact with the peasantry: the world of the country clergymen and backwoods squireens who went to Trinity to vote against Carson as˙ too liberal and Lecky as irreligious. 'An Craobhin Aoibhinn' rejected the beliefs of his father; yet behind the Gaelic Leaguer's attacks on Mahaffy echoes the Rev. Arthur Hyde cursing Trinity for making his sons agnostics.[5]

MacNeill's experience of the Scots Gaelic heritage of the Glens of Antrim led him to see the Ulster Protestants as 'really' Gaelic and Gaelic only; he dismissed the British, Protestant and Unionist aspects of their identity as delusions implanted by manipulative elites. As Minister for Education he forced Protestant schools to make Irish compulsory despite the opposition of teachers, parents, and pupils. Hyde supported this policy; Moran applauded it. At the same time MacNeill opposed compulsory education as an invasion of parental rights.[6] The 'Gaelic League as a whole believed that 'the Gael must be the element that absorbs'; Moran was simply more honest about how far this required the forcible repression of the Anglo-Irish tradition.

Similar confusion is visible in most who tried to reconcile the two traditions. William O'Brien made immense efforts in the cause of reconciliation, but his glaring personality defects helped to defeat him. Griffith pointed out the bigotry behind Moran's dismissal of Grattan and Davis; but his image of Unionist identity was as illusory as that of MacNeill. The only people who made any serious attempt to work out how the two traditions might be reconciled were small groups of intellectuals associated with Redmond and Horace Plunkett, and they could not secure mass support.

CONCLUSION 55

Moran's reaction to Protestant extremists, and their response to his reaction, fuelled the process of mutual escalation which destroyed the moderates; but again Moran was a representative rather than an initiator. He represented his fellow-nationalists both in willingness to accept the British Empire when there seemed no alternative, and adoption of separation when the First World War showed the full cost of the British link; but this was not necessarily 'moderation'. The censorship mentality, the political bitterness and cultural chauvinism bred by centuries of ascendancy and economic privilege, were evident before 1914, and a Home Rule government would have had to come to terms with them; given the intransigence of the Ulster Unionists and the widespread hostility towards the commercial and political influence of the small Southern minority in 1922–32, a thirty-two-county state with a large minority would have faced serious difficulties. One does not have to idealise the Anglo-Irish tradition to see that in trying to suppress it Moran and his contemporaries were engaging in cultural self-mutilation.

Moran's most valuable characteristics were his commitment to debate, the acuteness of his observations, and his business enterprise. He contrasts strikingly with the image of the Catholic nationalist as rural traditionalist; he would probably have called de Valera's 'comely maidens' speech '*ráiméis*'. He had the detached intelligence of a city boy. His sneers at mindless romanticism, his emphasis on human capital, his calls for a political realignment based on economic issues have a startlingly modern ring. It is not surprising that he admired Séan Lemass. His central project was the synergic linking of cultural revivalism, Catholic pride and an enterprise mentality; he wanted Catholic puritanism to perform the role of industrialising Ireland, which was sometimes attributed to its Protestant counterpart in industrialising Europe.

Moran's economic rationality blinded him to the extent to which Irish life and attitudes (including his own) were influenced by the romantic nationalist emotionalism he had rejected. Moran regularly referred (usually accurately) to positions he took over the years and tried to reconcile them with his present standpoint. This is stimulating, but often suggests an attempt to rationalise intuitive decisions. The editorial voice had a certain cost for the private Moran, whose views it both expressed and concealed.

The protectionism Moran advocated had the consequences he feared. Dark Brothers, Mean Brothers and cultural revivalists grew fat and complacent—until the floods came. Little Irelandism was not enough, and the new modernisers adopted an ideology very different from Moran's.

Moran's importance rests on his influence on his own generation, his commentary on the events of his lifetime, and *The Leader*'s role as a forum for debate. The period between the fall of Parnell and the Easter Rising was crucial in the making of modern Ireland, and those who feel its hopes and tensions will always benefit from the light shed by that baleful star.

NOTES

(References to *The Leader* are by date only)

1

[1] Obituary, *Waterford News*, 7 Feb. 1936. Several secondary sources claim that Moran was born in 1871, but his newspaper obituaries say he was born in 1869.

[2] *Irish Book Lover*, Sept. 1915; Stephen Brown, S.J., *Ireland in Fiction*, (rev. ed., Dublin, 1919), i, 216–17.

[3] 'Hibernicus' (Fr J. S. Sheehy), 22 Feb. 1936; Joseph A. Moran, 25 Apr. 1936.

[4] 'X' (D. P. Moran), 'Confessions of a Converted West Briton', 8 Sept. 1900; 3 Mar. 1928 (O'Brien); D. P. Moran, *Tom O'Kelly* (Dublin, 1905), pp. 224–6.

[5] 'Confessions of a Converted West Briton'; D. P. Moran, *The Philosophy of Irish Ireland* (Dublin, 1905), p. 13.

[6] *Irish Peasant*, 26 May 1906.

[7] 2 Feb., 29 Mar. 1924, 26 Oct. 1929 (Webb and Smith); 21 Mar. 1931 (editor); Nuala Moran in Golden Jubilee Issue, 21 Oct. 1950.

[8] 'Confessions of a Converted West Brition'.

[9] Piaras Béaslaí, 'Memories of D. P. Moran', Diamond Jubilee Issue, 3 Dec. 1960.

[10] Joseph A. Moran, 25 Apr. 1936.

[11] 16 July 1904.

[12] *An Claideamh Soluis*, 8 Apr., 3 June, 7 Oct. 1899.

[13] Golden Jubilee Issue, 21 Oct. 1950 (recollections by Nuala Moran); Séamus Ó Braonain, 'Sixty Years Ago—Almost', Diamond Jubilee Issue, 3 Dec. 1960.

[14] Donal McCartney, 'Hyde, D. P, Moran and Irish Ireland' in F. X. Martin (ed.), *Leaders and Men of the Easter Rising* (London, 1967), p. 47; Ruth Dudley Edwards, *Patrick Pearse: The Triumph of Failure* (London, 1977), pp 31–5, 42–4.

[15] Stanislaus Joyce, *My Brother's Keeper* (New York, 1958), p. 169.

[16] Hyde, quoted in Michael Tierney, *Eoin MacNeill* (Oxford, 1980), p. 59.

[17] 3 Sept. 1932.

2

[1] 22 Sept., 6, 20 Oct. 1900.

[2] 11 Mar. 1905.

[3] *An Claideamh Soluis*, quoted by Moran, 17 Jan. 1903.

[4] 18, 25 Mar., 1, 29 Apr. 1905.

[5] 18 Jan. 1902, 11 Dec. 1909.

[6] Moran, *Tom O'Kelly*, ch. 16.

[7] Obituary, 3 Sept. 1927.

[8] 23 Dec. 1922, 19 Apr. 1930.

[9] 16 Feb. 1907, (Parnell fantasy); obituary, 22 Sept. 1934.

[10] Richard Ellmann, *James Joyce* (rev. ed., Oxford, 1982), pp 70–73; C. P. Curran, *James Joyce Remembered* (Oxford, 1968), pp 16–17.

[11] William Dawson, 'Arthur Clery', *Studies*, xxii, no. 85 (Mar. 1933), pp 77–88; Arthur Clery, review of Hilaire Belloc, *The Jews* in *Studies*, xi, no. 44 (Dec. 1922), pp 648–50.

[12] T. MacF., 'Arthur Clery', 21, 28 Nov. 1942; Clery, 3 Dec. 1927.

58   D. P. MORAN

[13] Joyce, *My Brother's Keeper*, pp 141, 165–6; Curran, *James Joyce Remembered*, pp 16–17.

[14] Corkery's contributions are discussed in more detail in Patrick Maume, *'Life that is Exile': Daniel Corkery and the Search for Irish Ireland* (Belfast, 1993).

[15] *Waterford News* 7 Feb. 1936; Fogarty letter in Silver Jubilee Issue, 26 Sept. 1925; 13 Jan. 1912.

[16] 10 Oct. 1925, 6 June, 15 Aug. 1931.

[17] Obituary, 7 June 1923; *Catholic Bulletin*, Aug. 1923.

[18] Most recently by Brian P. Murphy, 'The Canon of Irish Cultural History: Some Questions', *Studies*, xxvii, no. 305 (spring 1988), pp 75–7.

[19] 8, 15, 22, 29 Dec. 1906, 5, 12, 19, 26 Jan. 1907.

[20] E.g. 10 June 1911, 17 Aug. 1912; Ernest Gellner, *Nations and Nationalism* (Oxford, 1983).

[21] Evelyn Bolster, *The Knights of St Columbanus* (Dublin, 1979).

[22] 20 Apr. 1907 (prediction); 19 July 1924 (fulfilment).

[23] 'George A. Birmingham', *Hyacinth* (London, 1906), pp 226–30.

[24] Frederick Ryan, *Criticism and Courage* (Dublin, 1906), pp 30–31.

[25] Alvin Jackson, 'The Failure of Unionism in Dublin', *Irish Historical Studies*, xxvi, no. 104 (Nov. 1989), pp 377–95.

[26] 27 May 1905.

[27] 'Arthur Synan', 'The Outlanders of Ulster', *New Ireland Review*, Oct. 1905; Eoin MacNeill, *Shall Ireland Be Divided?* (Dublin, 1925); 'Chanel', *The Idea of a Nation* (Dublin, 1907).

[28] 18 Aug. 1906.

[29] 1 Sept. 1900.

[30] 29 Aug. 1931.

[31] *The Collected Letters of W. B. Yeats*, iii: *1901-1904*, ed. John Kelly and Ronald Schuchard (Oxford, 1994).

[32] 3 Oct. 1903.

[33] 27 Sept. 1932 (dinner with Moore); 9 Apr. 1932 ('half-baked Orangeman'); Clery review of Page Dickenson, 'The Dublin of Yesterday', *Leader*, 7 Feb. 1931; 15 Feb. 1908; 24 Sept., 8, 15, 22 Oct. (controversy with AE).

[34] 28 Mar. 1932.

[35] Obituary, 27 Jan. 1923.

[36] 1 Apr. 1905; Clery's hopes for the theatre, 7 Jan. 1906.

[37] 2, 9 Feb. 1907, 3 June 7, 14, 21, 28 Oct. 1911, 30 Mar. 1912.

[38] Conor Cruise O'Brien, *Ancestral Voices* (Dublin, 1994), pp 82–3.

[39] Robert Hogan and James Kilroy, *The Modern Irish Drama*, iii: *The Abbey Theatre: The Years of Synge, 1905–1909* (Dublin, 1978), pp 10–15 (Griffith and Zaza), pp 148–9 (Sheehy Skeffington and Cruise O'Brien).

[40] 16 Sept. 1911.

[41] 15 Dec. 1923.

[42] C. H. Rolleston, *Portrait of an Irishman: T. W. Rolleston* (London, 1939), pp 118–19.

[43] 11 Apr. 1903.

[44] Arthur Griffith, *The Resurrection of Hungary* (3rd ed., Dublin, 1918), p. 10.

[45] J. B. Lyons, *The Enigma of Tom Kettle* (Dublin, 1983), pp 65, 77; 8 July 1911.

[46] Hence the guilt expressed by Conor Cruise O'Brien (*Ancestral Voices*, pp 50–52) about his father's contributions is misplaced.

[47] 10, 17 Feb. 1912.

NOTES   59

[48] Golden Jubilee Issue, 21 Oct. 1950.
[49] 'Imaal' obituary, 3 Sept. 1927.
[50] 10 Aug. 1907, 6 July 1931.

3

[1] 4 Nov. 1911.
[2] *Catholic Bulletin*, Jan. 1911.
[3] 11 Nov. 1911.
[4] 9, 16, 30 Dec. 1911.
[5] 20 Feb. 1909, 9, 16 Dec. 1911, 13 Apr. 1912, 6 June 1914.
[6] 3, 12 Dec. 1910, 28 Jan., 11 Feb. 1911.
[7] 3 Jan. 1914.
[8] 29 June 1912, 8 Feb. 1913.
[9] 16 Nov. 1912, 19 Apr., 17 May, 5, 26 July 1913.
[10] 1, 29 Mar. 1913.
[11] 11 Nov., 2, 9, Dec. 1911, 20, 27 Jan., 20 Apr., 9 Nov. 1912 (cartoon and verse); *Catholic Bulletin*, Nov. 1912.
[12] 13, 20 July, 3, 10, 17, 24, 31 Aug. 1913.
[13] James Loughlin, *Gladstone, Home Rule and the Ulster Question, 1882–93* (Dublin, 1986), pp 148–51. Rigg's articles begin 5 Oct. 1912.
[14] 14 Sept., 19 Oct. 1912.
[15] E.g. 30 Sept. 1911.
[16] 1 Nov. 1913.
[17] 6, 13, 20 Apr. 1912, 25 Oct., 8 Nov. 1913.
[18] 23, 30 Aug. 1913.
[19] F. X. Martin, 'MacNeill and the Foundation of the Irish Volunteers' in F. X. Martin and F. J. Byrne (eds.), *The Scholar Revolutionary: Eoin MacNeill, 1867–1945, and the Making of the New Ireland* (Shannon, 1973), pp 135, 138, 142.
[20] 9 Apr. 1910, 3 Jan. 1914.
[21] 2, 9 May 1914.
[22] 1 Aug. 1914.
[23] 8, 15, 22, 29 Aug. 5, 12, 19, 26 Sept., 3 Oct. 1914.
[24] Mabel Fitzgerald to G. B. Shaw, 7 Dec. 1914, in *The Memoirs of Desmond Fitzgerald*, ed. Garret Fitzgerald (London, 1968), p. 189.
[25] E.g. 21 June 1913.
[26] Breandan Mac Giolla Choille (ed.), *Intelligence Notes, 1913–16* (Dublin, 1966), p. 116.
[27] Piaras Béaslaí, 'Memories of D. P. Moran', Diamond Jubilee Issue, 3 Dec. 1960; 30 Oct., 13, 20 Nov. 1915.
[28] 26 June, 3 July, 21 Aug., 23 Oct. 1915; see also Arthur Clery, *Dublin Essays* (Dublin, 1920).
[29] 22 Aug. 1914.
[30] 3, 17, 24, June, 1, 8, 15, 22, 29 July, 19, 26 Aug. 9, 16, 23, 30 Sept. 7, 14, 21, 28 Oct., 11, 18, 25 Nov., 2, 9, Dec. 1916. A similar debate (on a smaller scale) took place when the first partition compromise was put forward by the government in 1914.
[31] E.g. 22, 29 Jan., 11 Mar., 1 Apr. 1916.
[32] 14 Apr., 5, 12 May 1917.
[33] 28 Mar. 1925.

60 D. P. MORAN

[34] 'Armagh Virumque', 9 Feb. 1918.

[35] 24 Dec. 1927.

[36] 16 Dec. 1933.

[37] Golden Jubilee Issue, 21 Oct. 1950.

[38] 1 Feb. 1930.

[39] Mary Kotsonouris, *Retreat from Revolution: The Dáil Courts, 1920–24* (Dublin, 1994) describes Clery's judicial career.

[40] 15 Nov. 1919 (cartoon); 29 Nov., 6 Dec. 1919 (Magennis); 14 Feb. 1919 (farmers' ball).

[41] 21 Aug., 18 Sept. 1920 (boycott), 15 Oct. 1921.

[42] 23 July, 27 Aug. 1921.

[43] 17 Dec. 1921, 12 July 1930 ('Devil's Sacrament'). For his flippancy see controversy with 'Irish-American', 17 May 1924 – 28 Mar. 1925.

[44] 14 Jan. 18, 25 Mar. 1922.

[45] 29 Apr., 6 May 1922.

[46] 20 Jan. 1923.

4

[1] 3 Sept. 1921 (anti-tariff), 7, 21, 28 Apr. 1923 (pro-tariff), 1 Mar. 1924 (cartoon).

[2] 29 Dec. 1923, 2, 16 Feb., 22 Mar. 1924, 4 Apr., 22 Nov. 1925.

[3] 21 Feb., 11 Apr. 1925.

[4] 16 Feb. 1929.

[5] 9 May 1925, 23 July 1927.

[6] 20 July 1929.

[7] 21 June 1924. This witticism was copied by Tim Healy after the commission collapsed.

[8] 'M.S.', 4 Dec. 1926.

[9] 3 June 1922, 7 July 1923, 2 Apr. 1927.

[10] 20 Aug. 1927, 21 Jan. 1928.

[11] Most famously by F. S. L. Lyons, *Culture and Anarchy in Ireland, 1890–1939* (Oxford, 1982): see Margaret O'Callaghan's criticisms in 'Language, Nationality and Cultural Identity in the Irish Free State, 1922–7: The *Irish Statesman* and the *Catholic Bulletin* Reappraised', *Irish Historical Studies*, xxiv, no. 94 (Nov. 1984), pp 226–45.

[12] 20 June 1925.

[13] 6, 20 Feb. 1926.

[14] 27 Oct. 1928.

[15] 26 Dec. 1925, 2 Jan. 1926.

[16] Cartoon 'The Farmer T.D.', 31 May 1924; see also Moran's comments, 24 May 1931.

[17] P. J. Fanning, a Gorey farmer (12 July 1924), and P. Bradley, a retired customs officer (29 Jan. 1927). Fanning later became a protectionist (20 Aug. 1932).

[18] E.g. 8 June 1929 (Clery predicts a new Union); 17 Jan. 1934 ('worshipping the bones'); 16 Feb. 1924 (Clery on foreign games).

[19] 3 Apr., 28 Aug. 1926, 26 Mar., 21, 28 May, 11, 18 June 1927.

[20] 19 Mar. ('Imaal'), 30 Apr., 18 June, 10 Sept. 1927, 21 Apr. 1928.

[21] 11 Nov., 16 Dec. 1922, 27 July, 3 Aug. (high wage policy) 1929, 29 Dec. 1934.

[22] 29 Apr., 1 July 1933.

NOTES

61

[23] 23 Jan., 20 Mar. 1926.

[24] Obituary, 21 Jan. 1928.

[25] 16 Feb. 1929; obituary, 6 Oct. 1934.

[26] 4 May 1929.

[27] 11 Oct. 1924.

[28] 26 Nov., 3 Dec. 1932, 25 Nov. 1933; William Dawson, 'Arthur Clery', *Studies*, xxii, no. 85 (Mar. 1933), pp 77–88.

[29] 18 May 1929.

[30] 21 July, 11 Aug. 1928.

[31] 11 Feb. 1928, 28 Sept. 1929.

[32] 27 Feb. 1932.

[33] 22 Oct., 26 Nov. 1932.

[34] 22 July, 5 Aug., 9 Dec. 1933 (Sweetman).

[35] E.g. 4 June 1927.

[36] 9 Dec. 1933.

[37] E.g. 21 Oct. 1933, 8 Sept. 1934; see also Moran on the shortcomings of dictatorship, 25 Aug. 1934.

[38] 12 Oct. 1935.

[39] 3 Mar., 7 Apr., 5, 12, 19 May 1934.

[40] P. Bradley, 17, 24 Mar. 1934.

[41] 24 Feb., 21 Apr. 1934.

[42] E.g. 2, 30 Sept. 1933.

[43] 12, 19, 26 Aug., 23 Sept. 1933.

[44] 27 Jan. 1934, 16 Dec. 1933.

[45] 7 July 1934.

[46] 29 Sept., 6 Oct. 1934.

[47] 30 Mar. 1935 (see also 30 June 1934).

[48] Extensive obituaries and tributes, 8, 15, 22 Feb. 1936 (further material 7, 14, 28 Mar., 11, 25 Apr., 9 May, 20 June 1936).

[49] Patrick Kavanagh, *Collected Pruse* (London, 1967), pp 163–219.

[50] J. J. Lee, *Ireland, 1912–85: Politics and Society* (Cambridge, 1989), p. 590.

Conclusion

[1] O'Brien, *Ancestral Voices*, pp 32–91.

[2] See Sean O'Faolain, *King of the Beggars* (Dublin, 1980 ed.), esp. pp 181–2.

[3] Douglas Hyde, 'The Return of the Fenians / Filleadh na Feinne' in Lady Gregory (ed.), *Ideals in Ireland* (London, 1901). The English mind is compared to a giant crow overshadowing Ireland and blotting out the sun. Moran also contributed to this volume. For the ideological relationship between Hyde and Moran see Margaret O'Callaghan, 'Moran and the Irish Colonial Condition, 1891–1921' in D. G. Boyce *et al.* (eds), *Political Thought in Ireland since the Seventeenth Century* (London, 1993), pp 146–60, esp. p. 148.

[4] Philip O'Leary, *The Prose Literature of the Gaelic Revival, 1891–1921* (Pennsylvania State University Press, 1994), pp 42–4, 215, argues convincingly against over-hasty attribution of Moran's attitudes to the movement as a whole.

[5] Dominic Daly, *The Young Douglas Hyde* (Dublin, 1974), p. 15.

[6] 11 July 1925 (Hyde speech), 15 Aug. 1925 (MacNeill speech), 26 Sept. 1925 (MacNeill article). Not all Gaelic Leaguers took this attitude: see 3 Oct. 1925 for Agnes O'Farrelly and George Moonan. E. Brian Titley, *Church, State and the Control of Schooling in Ireland, 1900–44* (Dublin, Kingston & Montreal, 1983), p. 92.

SELECT BIBLIOGRAPHY

Primary Sources

The most accessible statements of Moran's thought are *The Philosophy of Irish Ireland* (Dublin, 1905) and *Tom O'Kelly* (Dublin, 1905). Useful works by contributors are: Arthur Clery, *The Idea of a Nation* (Dublin, 1907) and *Dublin Essays* (Dublin, 1920); 'Imaal' [J. J. O'Toole], *Excursions in Thought* (Dublin, 1921; rev. ed. 1924); Michael O'Riordan, *Catholicity and Progress in Modern Ireland* (London, 1905); Louis J. Walsh, *Yarns of a Country Attorney* (Dublin, 1917), *Twilight Reveries* (Dublin, 1924) and '*Our Own Wee Town*' (Dublin, 1928). The fiftieth and sixtieth anniversary numbers of *The Leader* contain valuable recollections of Moran. Dawson's obituary for Clery (*Studies*, March 1933) and two articles by T. MacF. marking the tenth anniversary of Clery's death (*Leader*, 21, 28 November 1942) deserve a special mention.

J. J. Horgan, *Parnell to Pearse* (Dublin, 1948) and Leon Ó Broin, *Just Like Yesterday* (Dublin, 1986) are useful memoirs by *Leader* contributors. James Meenan (ed.), *Centenary History of the Literary and Historical Society of University College, Dublin* (Tralee, 1955) and Constantine Curran, *Under the Receding Wave* (Dublin, 1970) give accounts by contemporaries of the 'L. & H.' milieu and some *Leader* contributors. C. S. Andrews, *Dublin Made Me* (Dublin, 1979) describes the attitudes which led his father to subscribe to *The Leader*; Clery appears in the sequel, *Man of No Property* (Dublin, 1982).

Contemporary criticisms are expressed in Frederick Ryan, *Criticism and Courage* (Dublin, 1906), 'George A. Birmingham' [J. O. Hannay], *Hyacinth* (London, 1906), and M. J. F. MacCarthy *Rome in Ireland* (London, 1904).

Secondary Material

There is no full-length study of Moran, but the following are useful: Brian Inglis, 'Moran of *The Leader* and Ryan of *The Irish Peasant*' in Conor Cruise O'Brien (ed.), *The Shaping of Modern Ireland* (London, 1960); Donal McCartney, 'Hyde, D. P. Moran

SELECT BIBLIOGRAPHY   63

and Irish Ireland' in F. X. Martin (ed.), *Leaders and Men of the Easter Rising* (London, 1967); Patrick Callan, 'D. P. Moran, Founder Editor of *The Leader*' in *Capuchin Annual* (1977); William J. Feeney, 'D. P. Moran's *Tom O'Kelly* and Irish Cultural Identity', *Éire–Ireland* (fall, 1986); Margaret O'Callaghan, 'Denis [*sic*] Patrick Moran and the Irish Colonial Condition, 1891–1921' in D. G. Boyce, Robert Eccleshall and Vincent Geoghegan (eds), *Political Thought in Ireland since the Seventeenth Century* (London, 1993).

John Hutchinson, *The Dynamics of Cultural Nationalism* (London, 1987) has a particularly useful account of Moran and his milieu. Tom Garvin, *Nationalist Revolutionaries in Ireland, 1858–1928* (Oxford, 1987) draws on *The Leader* in his analysis of the social tensions which produced Moran and so many other Irish Irelanders. Conor Cruise O'Brien, *Ancestral Voices* (Dublin, 1994) is stimulating but idiosyncratic. Lawrence MacBride, *The Greening of Dublin Castle* (Washington, D.C., 1991) uses *Leader* articles on civil service discrimination. There are also useful references to Moran in Ruth Dudley Edwards, *Patrick Pearse: The Triumph of Failure* (London, 1977), J. B. Lyons, *The Enigma of Tom Kettle* (Dublin, 1983), Virginia Glandon, *Arthur Griffith and the Advanced Nationalist Press* (New York, 1985), and Patrick Maume, *'Life that is Exile': Daniel Corkery and the Search for Irish Ireland* (Belfast, 1993). Evelyn Bolster, *The Knights of Columbanus* (Dublin, 1979) discusses the Catholic Association. Brian Girvin, *Between Two Worlds* (Dublin, 1989) and Mary Daly, *Industrial Development and Irish National Identity, 1922–36* (Dublin, 1992) describe the background to the protectionist lobby of the 1920s, while Paul Bew and Henry Patterson, *Séan Lemass and the Making of Modern Ireland, 1945–66* (Dublin, 1982) describe its eventual disintegration.